Walking In The Spirit Collection

ISBN- 13: 978-0-9970856-3-1
ISBN- 10: 0997085630
Ecclesia Publishing House LLC

Printed in the United States of America

Walking In The Spirit Collection

Volume One

Booklets 1-8: With excerpts from The Battle For Life, A Wonderful Change, I Am Determined To Know Christ! Jehovah-Elohim: The Counsel of His Will, and The Image of Jehovah-Elohim.

Copyright © 2011 By: Dr. Earl W. Lacy

Table of Contents

Other books by Dr. Earl Lacy

A Wonderful Change
I Am Determined To Know Christ!
Jehovah-Elohim: The Counsel of His Will
The Image of Jehovah-Elohim
The Battle For Life

CHAPTER ONE

The Person & Ministry Of The Holy Spirit

אלוהים רוח

"In the beginning God created the heaven and the earth. 2 And the earth was without form, and void; and darkness was upon the face of the deep. And the **Spirit of God** (Heb. ruach Elohim אלוהים רוח) moved upon the face of the waters" ---Gen. 1.1,2.

This is the first mentioning of the Holy Spirit in the Holy Bible, and it is concerning creation. From this point on, the Person and power of the Holy Spirit is known as the principle and only source of power God uses to accomplish His plans, purposes and pursuits; the Holy Spirit is God's Spirit also, and without Him, God would not have Eternal, perpetual Life, nor Omnipresence, Omniscience and Omnipotence. From this viewpoint we approach the subject of the Holy Spirit as the Spirit of the Son---Christ the Word also, therefore a Trinity with distinct functions---ministries and personalities.

Son of God

6 "Jesus said unto him, I Am the Way, the Truth, and the Life; no man comes unto the Father, but by Me. 10 I Am in the Father, and the Father in Me..."---Jn. 14.6 (KJV).

These were the words of the Savior of the World as He approached the end of His three and a half years of human ministry. Having loved those who were in the world He loved them to the end. Years of walking the dusty trails of Israel and her neighboring countries was coming to an end; He taught in the synagogues and told the people that the **Spirit of the Lord God** was upon Him, for He had anointed Him to preach, teach, heal the sick, cast out demons; but above all this---to prepare a people for the LORD, Jehovah-Elohim, the Father and Creator. The Name (reputation) of Jehovah-

Elohim was known by many of the Jewish people in Jesus' earthly pilgrimage; the works of the Holy Ghost was also known by them too; but they didn't personally know the Love of Christ. So Jesus, the Christ trudged through the Earth Realm to educate and bless them by revealing to them that He was the Word (Christ) whom God created the worlds through, and without Him was not anything made that was made.

And God so loved the world that He sent His only begotten Son, so that whosoever believes in Him would not perish, but have everlasting Life, and participate in the Marriage Supper of the Lamb of God.

Jesus proclaimed that He and Jehovah-Elohim are One. This was a truth that many found hard to believe and even offensive, since Jesus of Nazareth obviously looked like a man. He made many bold statements to the intent that people would believe on Him. Another statement was, "I Am the Way, the Truth and the Life…." He wasn't saying that He was a way, a truth, a life; but He was the only Way, the only Truth, and the only Life; no one could even talk to or ascend to Jehovah-Elohim the Father without going through Christ, the Son.

Jesus told them that God didn't have a son in the way that human beings have children; in eternity before all time He was not the Son of God. At that point He was the Word (Christ) and was with God and the Holy Spirit; when the Word became a human being is when the Father had His Son, born of the virgin Mary.

But now it was time to leave this world, whereby the Ministry of the third member of the Trinity could begin: The Holy Spirit. He told them that He would ask the Father to send another Comforter, the Holy Spirit to abide with them and be in them forever, to such as are truly Saved and endure to the end. In the Old Testament, the Holy Spirit was the same Person (s) who gloriously dwelled in the arch of the Covenant. He was grieved at the behavior of Israel, and one day He gloriously left the temple and went back to Heaven (Ezek. 10).

Now, the LORD has returned as promised to redeem a people for His inheritance, to strike a decisive blow against Satan and the dark rulers; and He would do this through the death of His beloved Son. When His hour had come, He prayed for His twelve disciples and for all of us who would later believe in Him, not that God would take us out of the world but to protect us from the evil one, and strengthen us by His Spirit so we wouldn't return to the bondage and slavery of the wicked one. Jesus further prayed the perfect will of Jehovah-Elohim:

That God would glorify Him with His own Presence, so that the Son would give glory to the Father; that the Son would in turn give Eternal Life to those of us who dwell in the valley of the shadow of death; and this Eternal Life would manifest the Name and eternal counsel of His will and purposes of God in us, and that the heart, Love and joy of the LORD would be realized in us too.

We being redeemed from the curse of the Law, are sealed and kept by and through the authority of His Name; to the intent that we are one as He and the Father are One. For it has always been the Father's kind intent that the same Agape Love wherewith He lavishly pours out on Christ in their perfect arrangement, He lavishly pours out this Love on us also; even as He loved Christ before the found-ation of the world and evermore. For in Christ dwells the fullness of the Godhead bodily.

23 "...the true worshiper shall worship the Father in Spirit and in truth: For the Father seeks such to worship Him. 24 God is Spirit; and they that worship Him must worship Him in Spirit and in truth"---Jn. 4.23,24 (KJV).

Jesus went down to Jacob's well in Samaria. There He met a woman and asked her for a drink of water. The woman was surprised to see Jesus, a Jew down in that region; Samaria was like the ghetto in a major city; Samaria was a region that no "righteous" Jew would be at. According to the Jewish tradition, the Samaritans were half-breeds, dogs, and unclean as swine. Yet, Jesus loved them; the Son of man trudged to Samaria. There were other wells which Jesus could've drank water from--but that woman wasn't at those wells. Neither did Jesus go down there to call this woman's sins to remembrance--there were plenty of sinners in Jerusalem and the surrounding areas.

He arrived to give her the Living Water, the Word, His Resurrection Anointing to release ministry into her life. Yes, she was a sinner---but so was everyone else. Jesus, being the sinless One, arrived to share His righteousness with an outcast. She, not being Jewish had no Covenant with God. But Jesus, Jehovah--the Covenant Maker stood before her and offered her the Living Water that would bring her into a covenant relationship with Himself and satisfy her spiritual thirst; "...whosoever drinks of the water that I shall give him shall never thirst; but the water that I shall give him shall be IN HIM a well of water springing up into everlasting life" (v.14).

When she asked for this Living Water, immediately the conversation advanced to the purpose Jesus came into her life: Worship---if the Samaritans held their peace and didn't worship Him the rocks in Samaria would cry out! The Father who knows the hearts of everyone, knew there was a veil, a curtain of prejudice needing to be torn from top to bottom; there was also a common misconception concerning righteousness, and the who, what, when, where, how and why in worshipping the Father.

Jesus confided in her; He told her He was the Messiah, Christ, the Anointed One; and the fullness of the time had come for the Samaritans---the outcasts---to know what He requires of all peoples; that He will be gracious unto them at the hearing of their praise. Everyone in the Physical Realm that has breath must praise the Lord, magnify and give thanks---worship from the human temple---not a mountain, building or city.

Because God is Spirit and Man was created in His image and likeness, he's also spirit. Anyone who worships God must worship Him with their spirit by the prompting of the Holy Spirit; for the Father is looking for people willing to humble themselves and be filled with His Spirit of praise, and present themselves as a living sacrifice, holy, which is our reasonable service.

As Born Again Christians, we often forget that we're spirit beings and capable of communicating with the Father of spirits---God. Within our human spirit is the Holy Spirit, and the Holy Spirit is God. God communicates with us by His Presence within our recreated human spirit; then the information or blessings are transmitted to our soul which houses the mind; now we can comprehend, understand or receive healing virtue.

We look up in the sky and pray to God, but the truth is that God also dwells in our spirit. He's not in an inaccessible, archangel-guarded lofty place, but inside our sometimes rebellious temple of flesh. It's a mind boggling mystery why God even dwells in such fragile containers. After salvation we must learn to Practice the Presence. This is done through applying our faith in the Word of God. He's always with and in us; so we consciously acknowledge His Presence in our daily devotion and speak to Him throughout the day; we pray silently and aloud, with worshipping songs of praise and lift Him up: He will come forth in Presence and power. When we pray or worship the Lord with our spirit, it's really the Holy Spirit prompting the action.

God uses our lips to pray, praise and worship Himself! It's also God who speaks healings, blessings and favor into the Physical Realm. This shouldn't surprise us, since He indwells us to advance His kingdom on earth. When we were Unsaved we had no inclination or desire to praise the Lord; now that we're saved, why do we desire it now?

It's the Presence and promptings of the Holy Spirit in Covenant with our soul and mind submitting to His voice; and the Holy Spirit says through our lips, Praise the Lord! God assist us in what and how to pray, then answers Himself by providing the petition.

This may sound like nonsense, but it's true. Remember, it's the Holy Spirit who helps us to pray; how can we not get what we need if the Holy Spirit---who is God---is doing the praying and is the Provider? Will He prompt us to pray and not deliver? Will God turn down His own requests? Nay--He doesn't play games, neither will He withhold any good thing from us.

"For as many as are led by the Spirit of God, they are the sons of God. The Spirit bears record with our spirit, that we are the children of God" (Romans 8.14,16).

It's the Spirit who verifies that we're the children of God. He also helps us to be children, and testifies in our spirit by revelation that Jesus Christ is the Lord, and we should listen to His Word.

The Holy Spirit gives us boldness. In the early church, the disciples were forbidden to speak in the Name of Jesus. The disciples assembled together and lifted up their voices to God in one accord, and said,

"And now, Lord, behold their threatening; and grant unto thy servants, that with all boldness they may speak Thy Word. By stretching forth Thy hand to heal; and that signs and wonders may be done by the Name of Thy holy child Jesus. And when they had prayed, the place was shaken where they assembled together, and **THEY WERE ALL FILLED WITH THE HOLY GHOST**, and they spoke the Word of God with boldness" (Acts 4.18-31).

The Holy Spirit (called the Holy Ghost to designate He's a Person) changes people and circumstances. Prayer is sanctioned communication with the Mighty One:

"Who, is clothed with honor and majesty; Who covers Himself with a garment of Light, and stretches out the heavens like a curtain; Who laid the beams of His chambers in the waters; Who makes the clouds His chariot, and walks upon the wings of the wind; Who makes angelic spirits and His ministers a flaming fire; Who laid the foundations of the earth, that it should not be moved forever" (Psalms 104.1-5).

This is the Holy Spirit we love and depend on to strengthen us. Again the power of God manifested in response to an Italian centurion named Cornelius. He was "A devote man, and one that feared God with all his house, which gave much alms to the people (sowed seed into the Kingdom of God), and prayed to God always."

And the Lord said to him, "Thy prayers and thy alms are come up for a memorial before God" (V.1,2,4). Marvelous! His prayers and charity to the poor was remembered and became the object of MEMORIAL before Him. It was something God couldn't ignore. Cornelius had been pressing into the Kingdom for a long time. He couldn't touch the heart of God because he wasn't Born Again; he needed the special grace that only Salvation, the indwelling of the

Holy Spirit could give him. Nevertheless, his alms caught God's eye.

This Gentile family would be visited by the Person and Resurrection Anointing of Jesus Christ; it's He who resurrects the spiritually dead. For it was predestined that the Blessing of Abraham would come upon the Gentiles through Jesus Christ. The Lord told Cornelius to send for the Apostle Peter, who would lead him to the throne of Grace. Simon Peter was no different than other Jews in regard to the Gentiles. He was prejudice and ignorant of God's "grafting in" plan concerning the Gentiles. The Holy Spirit spoke to him in a vision, then audibly, as he was on the roof in meditation. The main focus of the vision was revelation knowledge: God is no respecter of persons.

He told Peter, "Behold, three men seek thee. Arise therefore, and get thee down, and go with them, DOUBTING NOTHING: for I have sent them" (v.19,20). When Peter arrived, Cornelius fell down at Peter's feet and worshipped him. Peter panicked. He picked Cornelius up and told him that an apostle is a mere man--but the Lord Jesus Christ is worthy to be praised and adored!

It was against Jewish ordinances for Peter to be in Cornelius' house; obedience to the Holy Spirit is better than sacrifices and traditions. Both men were fasting and praying at their homes when the Holy Spirit contacted them. Neither man knew they were in one accord with the plan of God. The Spirit of God was walking throughout the earth searching for souls to worship the Lord.

After Peter preached the Word of Life, the Anointing fell upon the Gentiles. They were saved and **Baptized in the Holy Spirit with the scriptural evidence of speaking in tongues**. Now the Cornelius family could worship the Father in Spirit and in truth, because they possessed the Baptism in the Holy Spirit to usher them before the Presence of God.

"For one who speaks in an [unknown] tongue speaks not to men but to God, for no one understands or catches his meaning, because in the [Holy] Spirit he utters secret truths and hidden things [not obvious to the understanding]. He that speaks in a [strange] tongue edifies and improves himself..." (1 Cor. 14.2,4 Amp. Bible).

Many times we cannot perceive the Presence of Christ in our life because we expect to "feel" something with our external and soul-life senses. Often our attention, therefore our heart and treasure is in the world and the pleasures of participating in it. Fasting and prayer is the key to getting back on track; it's a sacrifice and offering to God; it humbles the soul (psyche life force) and weakens the strength of the physical (bio life force) by denying---even crucifying them, withdrawing the pleasures and comforts they love and depend on.

By this the regenerated human spirit housing the Holy Spirit (Zoe Life force) is exalted which brings us in His Presence. Faith is a bridge which transports us to where Christ sits upon the throne of our life. The situations and temptations of life can become a sweat-less victory if we would worship in the Spirit and let the Master Builder of creation solve our problems.

By divine right God rules creation; only with our permission can He be both Savior and Lord of our life. Praying in the Spirit is Christ expressing Himself in and through us to manifest His plans, purposes, and pursuits. As much as we want our child to take a bath, even more so does God wants His children to take a bath---be Baptized in the Holy Spirit and speak with tongues; and manifest His Spirit. This Anointing is on His blood; it's also on the Word and Name of Jesus: Jesus is God's righteousness revealed.

We must know Him and the power out-flowing from His resurrection. Through obedience, faithfulness to the promptings of the Holy Spirit, the supernatural Christ can solve our personal and social problems: The Holy Spirit desires to minister in the areas of drugs, violence, lawlessness in schools and streets, national and international crisis, sickness, hunger and poverty. The Spirit is compassionate concerning the plight of twentieth century Man: The plagues of AIDS, Ebola, Leprosy, Cancer, Criminality, Insanity, Suicide, Crack, and depression. He wants to help us rise up against the demonic spirits who are bent on murdering us.

The Holy Spirit is fire; He's always fired up. We're the ones who become lukewarm, cold, and say, "The Devil doesn't bother me. If we leave the Devil alone--don't even mention his name--he'll leave you alone." But the Devil is a murderer; he's aggressive, an oppressor, relentless, he master deceiver and father of lies. If he's not coming against us it's because he already has us:

We need to check our relationship with Christ. If there are no "difficulties" in life: When was the last time we witnessed for Christ, studied the Word o r prayed? When was the last time we attended church or Prayer Meeting? Are our tithes up to date? Is there someone we know in the hospital or jail that we haven't visited? If the Devil isn't bothering us we could be backslidden. Satan is the sworn enemy of God and His family. Satan has already stolen our terrestrial inheritance; we're only taking back what already belongs to us, and enforcing the victory won by Jesus Christ at Calvary.

Many saints live quiet, complacent yet defeated lives as they appease the Devil. We're radical people: Complacency comes at the expense of missing God, by not rendering to Him praise and worship. Praise and worship makes the Devil angry. If he comes against us we have authority to rebuke him in the Name of Jesus Christ. We must never cease to praise Jesus and bring down the glory cloud so thick that it chokes the Devil! He'll run away depressed with his spirit of depression. It's not our inheritance to live a defeated, miserable life; that's not victory in Jesus.

We may sing victory songs but true victory arrives when The Holy Spirit of prayer, praise and worship rises up in us, inspiring faith and obedience to Christ. This brings soundness of spirit, soul and body, the **wealthy place** that God predestined before the foundation of the world. Victory in Jesus is amazing Grace. His Grace manifests in His faithfulness to all generations.

Never has God wanted us to be sick, poor and oppressed. God is a good God, and the Devil is a bad Devil; it's not hard to figure out who is doing what to us! If we believe that its God's will for us to be oppressed by sickness and poverty, then why do we go to doctors to get healed? Wouldn't we be disobeying God? And why do we receive promotions, raises, and buy items on sale, if we believe it's God's will for us to be poor? Why invest in a 401 K Plan, stocks and bonds, if God gets pleasure out of His people being broke? People who claim to believe such things are usually the first in line at a million dollar lottery drawing!

They are lying hypocrites! Giving to God's cause is worship. If we have nothing to give how can we help those in need. God gives us the ability to get wealth so we can praise Him for and with it. Many of us have become too unreasonable---even un-teachable---and miss the Person of Jesus Christ and His inheritance. Remember, He incarnated into the Physical Realm to raise up the names of the dead---our name---upon our inheritance. The least we can do is praise and worship Him: Seek the Giver not the gift.

Holy Spirit in the Apostles

25 "And at midnight Paul and Silas prayed, and sang praises unto God; and the prisoners heard them. 26 And suddenly there was a great earth-quake, so that the foundations of the prison were shaken: and immediately all the doors were opened, and everyone's bands were loosed"--- Acts 16:25-26 (KJV).

As Paul and Silas traveled to spread the gospel, they encountered a slave girl who had an unclean spirit using her to speak into the Physical Realm; it was a spirit of divination. She introduced the apostles and their purpose for being in that city. But Paul wanted to socialize with the people and get to know them before preaching to them.

Never does the Lord use demonic spirits to prepare the way for Him; the Holy Spirit was grieved and rose up in Paul to rebuke the unclean spirit who announced that Jesus was the Christ; so Paul rebuked and cast out the evil spirit from her. Her masters lost their investment and edge in commerce by her foretelling the future. Immediately, the demonic kingdom focused their influence on the apostles. The people rioted, claiming the apostles taught customs that were unlawful for Romans to observe. The magistrates ripped the apostle's clothes off, beat them and threw them in prison. It didn't look to promising for the apostles. Under these circumstances, most of us would be infuri-ated, cursing, threatening lawsuits and accusing the people and officials.

We in Silas' place would say to Paul, "Look what you got me into! I'm bleeding to death and my outfit and reputation is ruined! It was your idea to preach to these crazy Gentiles! Paul---you missed it--- the Holy Spirit couldn't have told you to come here!" Throbbing pain would've caused many of us to lay there, conserve our strength and think up some legal maneuver or plea bargain to get out of jail. But Paul and Silas prayed and sang praises unto God; and the prisoners heard them. Yes, the apostles weren't humming or moaning Zion songs but actually singing, rejoicing from their hearts. Even the prisoners, knowing how themselves were whipped, who cursed and complained, thought the apostles were the toughest men on earth. Who are these strangers who when beaten sing songs? Who's the God they serve who enables them to love their enemies? The praise of the apostles was their testimony that Jesus is alive.

Their prayers and songs of praise were like two candles in that dark dungeon; the food was terrible, the conditions were inhuman, and the treatment was harsh---but in that corner of the dungeon hope emerged---Living Water flowed into the hearts of the prisoners and chased away the evil. They brought the Holy Fire.

The prison was shaken, the doors creaked open, the shackles snap- ped off of everyone's feet, and the yokes upon their souls were destroyed and the captives set free. Yet no one escaped from the dungeon. This made the jailer grateful, otherwise he would've killed himself. The gospel was preached and the jailer and his house- hold got Saved.

We should be the type of Christians it can be said: "These that have turned the world upside down are come hither also" (Acts 17.6). Truly our prayers, praises and worship can turn the world upside down if we will offer them. For out of our belly shall flow rivers of living waters--rivers of miracles from Him who lives forever: Glory to the Lamb of God!

Via Della Rosa, the way of suffering is also the life of Jesus of Nazareth. To know Him is to know of His suffering; it's to weep over the "Jerusalem" of every city and state; to groan and be troubled in our spirit when we encounter sickness, hunger, poverty, or inhuman ity. Contemplating upon His and our death upon the cross brings fresh revelations.

There are countless levels to knowing Christ; suffering with persecution for His cause is something we should be prepared to do; suffering, too, is our reasonable service. Yet many of us Christians want the benefits without the labor. We don't want to pay the price. We want the personal relationship and the Anointing of the Holy Spirit but not the "fellowship of Christ's suffering" that comes with it. We don't want the personal, supernatural, intimate, progressive relationship that Paul wrote about in Phil. 3.10-12. The Jesus Christ in the Bible, the historical Jesus, is all that we know of Him. He's the Unknown God. The Spirit of God flared inside the Apostle Paul and led him to the City of Athens, Greece. On arrival Paul found the city OVERTHROWN BY SPIRITS OF IDOLATRY; there was no better place for Paul to be; for the Holy Spirit used him mightily. Immediately, the philosophers and theologians brought Paul to the Aeropagus to hear his doctrine.

The Grecians spent a lot of time studying and debating old and new doctrines. The Holy Spirit prompted Paul to take notice of an inscription on an altar: TO THE UNKNOWN GOD. Paul reasoned that this inscription was an attempt by the religious leaders to know the Person of God: The Unknown God was honored just in case in the worship of the other gods, he would be excluded---or become jealous---even angry at them and his blessing would be missed.

The Unknown God was not the God of Israel; it was only one of several false gods. Nevertheless, Paul capitalized on the superstition of the Grecians to tell them about Jesus of Nazareth and Him being raised from the dead. The Grecians were amazed; they entertained the possibility of the resurrection of the dead and thought Paul worth hearing: How could a man named Jesus of Nazareth find favor with God and be raised from the dead?

The philosophers were accustomed to worshipping gods made out of natural materials; they had eyes but couldn't see; mouths they had but couldn't speak; hands had they but couldn't save; they also had legs and feet but couldn't walk---Certainly, Paul's God was worth investigating!

Moses told Israel, Take heed: "And lest thou lift up thy eyes unto heaven, and when thou see the sun, and the moon, and the stars, even all the host of heaven, should be driven [by Satan] to worship them, and serve them... Take heed unto yourselves, lest ye forget the covenant of the LORD your God, which He made with you, and make you a graven image, or the likeness of anything, which the LORD thy God hath forbidden thee" (Deu.4.19,23). Without the wooing and guidance of the Holy Spirit, are we worshipping the Unknown God like the Grecians?

Do we KNOW Jesus Christ as our Savior and Lord? Is it possible, highly probable, we've missed Him and found religion instead? These are serious questions we must honestly ask ourselves. The evidence that we're saved is the Presence of the Holy Spirit---Christ in us. His Presence manifests in us as a changed life.

Whereas, before we embraced sin, but now we loathe to sin. Before we praised ourselves and our material possessions---our plastic Visa god---but now we've exchanged them for the living God. Before we cursed God and frequented the host of heaven: Satan's cults, psychics, tarot readers, palm readers, religions, clubs---and ran from Jesus, the lover of our soul. Now we proclaim: "What a friend I have in Jesus!"

Regeneration

Regeneration is Salvation, the raising from spiritual death and our human spirit energized. There has to be a behavioral change: The wicked things we used to do we don't do anymore; the bars and parties we used to attend we don't attend anymore. Before we may have gone to church but our bible collected dust all week---that has also changed, because the Lord has made a great change in our life. Now we look forward to going to church, prayer meetings and bible studies.

Our selfish agenda has gone out the window; we were blind now we can see. We eagerly serve His plans, purposes and pursuits.

Through our faithfulness, we have become useful vessels fit for the Master's use. Having been filled unto overflowing capacity with His Spirit, we no longer are the human host for every unclean and hateful spirit. We aren't slaves to sin. The Lord Jesus Christ is unknown to a lot of people.

It is the Ministry of the Holy Spirit and we Christians, wherewith the love of Christ constrains us to win the lost at any cost. We can worship the Lord by winning souls into His kingdom. The one who wins souls is wise; and Christ is made unto us Wisdom and the power of God. Winning souls manifests the Presence, Person and Spirit of Christ. Witnessing is a form of worship. Paul went to Greece: Maybe we will never witness overseas, but we can finance those who do. We can finance missionary journeys similar to the ones Paul went on. Our unselfish sowing into the kingdom brings us closer to knowing the Giver of all life. "Let him who glories glory in this, that he understands and knows Me, that I AM the LORD" (Jer. 9.24). As a Christian: To know the Lord is also to know thyself.

"So too the {Holy} Spirit comes to our aid and bears us up in our weakness; for we do not know what prayer to offer nor how to offer it worthily as we ought, but the Spirit Himself goes to meet our supplication and pleads in our behalf with unspeakable yearnings and groaning too deep for utterance"--- Ro 8.26 (Amp. Bible).

Apostle Paul discovered: "I find then a Law, that, when I would do good, evil is present with me" (Rom 7.21). That statement sounds so terrible and haunting; and for the unsaved, rightly so. But we who have received the indwelling of the Person of the Holy Spirit, the third member of the Trinity, have another Law working to help us win the Battle for Life.

It is called the **Law of the Spirit of Life** that is in Christ Jesus. Through the Law of the Spirit, there is no condemnation, no judgment, and the arrest warrant is cancelled for those of us who have been translated into Christ Jesus, who no longer walk as the unregenerate, spiritually dead but are led, walk, live in the Spirit and newness of life.

We are therefore free from the **Law of Sin and Death**, the consequences and penalties of sin (but not immune to the out-working of another Spiritual Law called the Law of Reciprocity---sowing and reaping) as long as we do not rely on the animal nature and connection that the flesh has with the world rulers, but rely on the Spirit of God; then the righteous nature of the Law will be fulfilled in us. This is because in the flesh we cannot please God and our best works on our best days are but rotten, filthy rags, grave clothes that smell in His nostrils.

The Holy Spirit when given His course of action will heal and preserve our physical bodies to provide us with a long life and spiritual service that is acceptable to God our Father. For the true sons and daughters of God are those who are led by His Spirit; if we don't have His Spirit resident in us, God does not claim or accepts us into His Divine Family; because we are considered a tare (weed) among the precious grain, or goats that are driven but cannot be led. It is also the assignment and pleasure of the Holy Spirit to bear witness with our human spirit that we are the children of God. He tells us that we are heirs of God, joint heirs with Jesus Christ.

When the Holy Spirit enters our human spirit, our spirit recognizes Him and cries out Abba---Father. Our human spirit knows who its Father is, and for the first time since we exited our mother's womb the spirit within us feels adequate, loved and secure; before it was unconscious, comatose, unresponsive, collapsed upon itself and useless as far as assisting the soul and body in the Battle of and for Life; but Christ crucified changed that forever.

The whole creation groans and travails like a woman having a baby, while waiting for the sons of God to be revealed; creation is waiting for us, the Earthbound Church to get it together, do what God says, walk and live in the Spirit, so Jesus can come back to take us home. On that day will be the complete redemption of our bodies; we will receive the completion of our Salvation---what has not yet been worked out by and through the Agency of the Holy Spirit in conjunction with our participation and cooperation in the Word of God.

Glorification Day

This marks the end of the Sanctification Process, the end of the process that the Holy Spirit uses to renew our minds, cleanse us of sin and bad habits. On this day the Church will be presented to Jesus Christ by the Father as a chaste Bride, holy, obedient to her Husband and without spot or blemish.

We know that something inside is wrong; we struggle to do what the Word of God says but wind up doing the opposite; it is no longer us, our will being done but the old man using the Law of Sin and Death to have his way, to mount a coup and by force and violence take his throne back. The old man is like the "ites" that multiplied and almost ran Israel back out of the Promised Land. But fortunate for us, the Holy Spirit monitors the rest of us from His living quarters in our human spirit. He sees the schemes of the flesh and the demonic host, and moves us to pray in the Spirit, in other tongues, as He makes intercessions, definite and accurate petitions to the Father. He does this because we do not know how or what to pray for, nor do we know what the demonic scheme is, how, where, day or hour it will transpire.

God who monitors His own Spirit at all times, whether inside Himself or inside us, knows what the Holy Spirit thinks and feels at all times, as the Holy Spirit represents our welfare and the plans, purposes and pursuits of God.

Spirit of Life

"For the **Law of the Spirit of Life** in Christ Jesus hath made me free from the **Law of Sin and Death**"--- Ro. 8.2 (KJV).

The **Law of the Spirit of Life** is the highest law of God. It is the cohesive element, the Agape Love that binds the Trinity into one unity, moving as three-in-one but separate in personality and function; each Person regarding the other as Himself duplicated, and the Law of the Spirit of Life sustaining them all. As the Holy Spirit of God is the Life that keeps God alive, and makes Him eternal, so this same Spirit residing in us, is effective and active by Faith.

This Law of the Spirit is more than a conquer against the Law of Sin and Death. If God hadn't given us His Spirit by way of the obedience, death and resurrection of Jesus Christ, the entire human population of the world would have been destroyed like Sodom and Gomorrah; for when the stroke of punishment was due, God's wrath and righteous judgment fell full force upon Jesus. God declared in times past that the wages of sin is death.

Jesus Christ received the blow, the punishment for our sins; then on the day of Pentecost (Acts. 2.1) the Holy Spirit entered the world as the direct results of the Promise of the Father; with His entrance and indwelling came the authority of the Law of the Spirit of Life, to cancel the requirements of the Law of Sin and Death. So as we walk in the Spirit we will not fulfill the lust of the flesh; and if we are willing to be led by the Spirit we are no longer under the Law of Sin but under Grace. It is our choice, because the Law of Sin is not done away with if we choice to walk in it, neither is sin done away with if we chose to continue to sin and live a sinful lifestyle.

But to those of us who have reckoned ourselves dead to sin and its consequences, then the Law of the Spirit operates in us. Many of us religiously adhere to the notion that once Saved we can go back to our former sinful behaviors and that Grace will automatically cover us; this is called by many "**cheap grace**"; it is also presumptuous, premeditated sin, a **thinking distortion spirit**, to believe that either we will repent later or that Grace will automatically cover us; it's putting God to a foolish test.

Cheapening God's grace is a subtle, dangerous reasoning, the splitting of hairs, a perceived loop hole or grey area that promotes risky behavior; it causes us to frustrate the Grace of God and try God's patience; this is also the reasoning that many former and present day preachers have moral difficulties, but continue to preach and live sinful and often illegal lifestyles (theft and sexual offences) up to the day they are prosecuted and/or publicly exposed. For these preachers have forgotten the Word:

"Be not deceived God is not mocked: for whatever a man sows, that shall he also reap. For he that sows to his flesh shall of the flesh reap corruption; but he that sows to the Spirit shall of the Spirit reap Life everlasting" ---Gal. 6.8,9).

The Law of the Spirit of Life, through the Eternal Lord Jesus Christ, has blessed us on earth with spiritual blessings in heavenly places in Christ. Christ chose us to be a member of His Christian Family before the foundation of the world. He chose us and separated us from the masses to be a holy people. He also elected, predestinated and called us by His Grace through wisdom and prudence; and forgave us of our sins in order to express His compassion and Love during the dispensations of times, with His spiritual children.

He also left us an inheritance and a divine purpose-driven life, as He worked out all situations and circumstances from the end of time backwards to the beginning of time, according to the counsel of His own will. Those of us who trust in Jesus Christ, are sealed by the Holy Spirit; He is God's down payment and Promise that He will return and finalize the transaction of the purchased possession. Until then, we are to be led by the Spirit with the knowledge that we are in this world but not of it, that we are strangers and foreigners just passing through and not obligated or compelled to make our home here, under the watchful stare of the demonic spirits; but are to keep our eyes on the prize: The One who loves us and gave His life for us.

The Lord Jesus Christ has been made unto us Wisdom and spiritual insight. We experience and are in awe of the "exceeding greatness of His power to us that believe, according to the working of His mighty power, which He wrought in Christ, when He raised Him from the dead, and set Him at His own right hand in the heavenly places.

"Even when we were dead in sins, He has quickened us **together** with Christ (by grace you are saved) And has raised us up **together**, and made us sit **together** in heavenly places in Jesus Christ" (Eph. 1.19,20;2.5,6).

As the Father, Son, Holy Spirit sit "**together**" in One unity, so are we seated **together** in them. We are His workmanship, the fruit of His labor in the vineyard, the multiplied single Seed that fell to the earth and died, was buried and produced a multitude of spiritual offspring called Christians. He also planned and predestinated paths for us to walk in to fulfill His purpose and our appointed destinies which includes the Calling and Commission of Ministry Gifts.

Therefore, Jesus Christ is the Prince of Peace; He by the Holy Spirit placed our hand in God's hand so that we walk together in agreement. God in turn cancelled the indictment and spiritual warrant that was pending against us, because Christ has ripped in half the veil that separated us from God because of our sinfulness; and in so doing Christ reconciled us to God by defeating Satan and his not so subtle manipulation of the Law of Sin and Death against us, and thus Christ created a New Creature: A species of being that had never existed before in Heaven or on earth: A Christian.

Therefore the Spirit of Life is the foundation of God, who makes us a habitation of God through the Spirit; a building whose found-ation rest upon and are built up on the apostles and prophets, Jesus Christ being the Chief Cornerstone; and because of this we are "strengthened with might by His Spirit in the inner man; that Christ may dwell in your hearts by faith; that ye, being rooted and ground-ed in love" (Eph. 3.16,17), may know the Person of Jesus Christ.

Through the Spirit we are not only rooted and grounded in the Love of Christ, but He also gave **Ministry Gifts** to the Church: **Apostles, prophets, evangelists, pastors and teachers** for the maintaining and building up of the Body of Christ, until everyone is strong in the Lord and in the power of His might; we are no longer tossed to and fro by human or demonic doctrines, religions or philosophies, or the pleasures of the flesh.

"For ye are dead, and your life is hid with Christ in God" (Col. 3.3). 15 "Do not love or cherish the world or the things that are in the world. If anyone loves the world, love for the Father is not in him. 16 For all that is in the world---the lust of the flesh {cravings for sensual gratification} and the lust of the eyes {greedy longings of the mind} and the pride of life {assurance in one's own resources or in the stability of earthly things}---these do not come from the Father but are from the world {itself}"---1Jn. 2.15,16 (Amp. Bible).

Many honest Christians observe with dismay, "I don't feel dead; I am very much alive and sin every now and then!" The Scriptures do not say that when we receive Salvation and the Holy Spirit indwells us that we immediately stop sinning; if this were the case, 1 John 1.9 would make no sense: "If we confess our sins, He is faithful and just and will forgive us our sins and purify us from all unrighteousness." This verse was written to the Christian Churches----not the local tavern.

However, in our Christian life there should be a gradual decrease in sin as we mature in Christ. If there is no decrease in sin due to the renewing of the mind by the Holy Spirit, it is likely that we are not converted, but have a religious or emotional experience, a mental assent to the truth of the Gospel, but no actual heart acceptance and conversion; we need to search the Scriptures.

The Apostle John further declared the Gospel according to what he and the other apostles saw with their eyes, heard with their ears, and participated in the Word of Life, who is Jesus Christ. He touched Jesus, the Word of God, and He is a real Person; and this Eternal Life (Holy Spirit) provided John and the other apostles with fellowship with the Father, Jehovah-Elohim. John proclaimed that God is Light and there is no darkness in Him. John stated earlier that in Jesus Christ was Life and the Life was the Light of the world.

So in the same way that there is no darkness or wickedness in Christ, the ideal lifestyle is there be no wickedness in us, no running errands for the Devil either!

If we walk in the Spirit of Christ we truly have fellowship with Him, and our Spiritual Gifts and Fruit of the Spirit reflect the authority, personality and character of Jesus Christ, whose Blood already cleansed us from all sins, so all we have to do is accept this as fact and not theory (doubt/unbelief) then live according to it, reckon ourselves already dead to sin but alive in Christ.

To say that we walk in the Spirit as Christians and love the Life/Light and don't do what the Word says is being a hypocrite and living in the darkness, a shady and shallow existence influenced by this evil world; and those who say that they love Christ but hate others are liars too (1 Jn. 2.9).

Liars do not go to Heaven. John further instructed that the world and everything in it is not to be loved. He is not referring to the people of the world which we must love spiritually and unconditionally. All of us can easily think of someone we do not particularly like and therefore fail to love them; but the love of the world produces dependency on the world which leads to bondage and slavery by those who control the world operations, economy, laws, morals and acceptable behaviors.

What may be State, Supreme Court legal or acceptable behavior to society could grieve the Holy Spirit of God---be blatant sin to God. John stated that we who love the world, the love of the Father isn't in us.

Seven-Fold Meaning of Comforter

"And he asked them, Did you receive the Holy Spirit when you believed {on Jesus as the Christ}? And they said, No, we have not even heard that there is a Holy Spirit" Acts 19.2 (Amp. Bible).

At Ephesus, the Apostle Paul came upon "Believers" who had not received the Holy Spirit. The obvious reason why they had not received Him was because they did not know that He exists as a divine Person who is willing to indwell and lead them.

Not long ago, I (Author) attended two local churches and for a moment thought I was in Ephesus amongst Believers who did not receive the Holy Spirit; they did not know that the Holy Spirit is a Person and member of the Godhead. So instead of praise, worship, and joy in the Holy Ghost, they had a dry "Devotion" segment, a form of godliness, legalism, printed programs, heaviness and despair.

When the pastor preached, I heard him refer to the Holy Spirit as an "it", which implied the pastor didn't have an intimate knowledge or relationship with Him, no revelation of His greatness, authority and leadership; and so he could not bring his congregation into the fullness of worshipping Jesus Christ.

Jesus referred to the Holy Spirit as the Comforter (Jn. 16.7. Comforter has a seven-fold meaning:

1. As **our Helper**, the Holy Spirit assists us from His residence within our human spirit. He helps us live the Christian lifestyle. He also helps us to pray because we don't know how or what to pray for. The Holy Spirit knows our needs and **prays according to the Father's predestined plan** for our lives; our prayers are harmonized.

2. As our **Comforter**, He keeps us at peace in trials, tribulations, bereavement and loneliness. He has **genuine feelings and perceptions.** He is aware of any change in our consciousness. He moves to comfort and undergird us with Himself, thus bringing us through the valleys in our lives.

3. As **our Counselor**, He leads us into the Truth (In Him---Jesus). He opens our understanding to the Word of God. The Holy Spirit is the Author of the Holy Bible; He is its Holy Interpreter, who gives us scriptural advice. The Counselor instructs us in the paths of righteousness. He tutors us because we are the King's sons and daughters; and we must learn the ways of our Father. But the Holy Spirit will not make us accept His advice. He will not cancel our free will, the right to chose.

4. As **our Advocate**, He pleads our cause before the Father. The Holy Spirit is the Spirit of God the Father and God the Son. As God the Holy Spirit, He is sent here to **fellowship with us**. He is responsible for our spiritual, emotional, intellectual, physical and material needs.

5. As **our Intercessor**, the Holy Spirit puts our hand in the Father's hand through the Lord Jesus Christ. He is also the **Spirit of Adoption**, the One who adopts us into the Family of God. As Intercessor, He is **our lifetime Prayer Partner**, the lifeline to the

Lord Jesus Christ; He ushers us into His Presence, praying with groaning, while searching our hearts and revealing them to the Godhead; and searches God's heart and reveals His thoughts and desires to us.

6. As **our Strengthener, He gives us power to resist temptations**. He brings to our remembrance what the Word of God says, sends visions, heavenly dreams, speaks audibly to us, reminds us of forgotten experiences and con-sequences of the past that will assist us to make present-day choices and live victoriously. He gives us **courage and boldness to be witnesses for Jesus Christ**. He restores our souls, renews our minds and heals our bodies.

7. As **our Standby**, the Holy Spirit is the Greater One within us. **He has our back**. He is the power of the Godhead behind our words when we invoke the Name of Jesus. We command evil spirits to leave and they obey. He watches and protects us from seen and unseen dangers. **The Holy Spirit gives us Spiritual Gifts**, and calls us into His Ministry.

Summary

The Holy Spirit is our Comforter and Companion in life; He is in charge of our Sanctification and mind renewal; He also prays, intercedes for us, interprets and translates the answer from God, and reveals to us what the Word of God says so that we can obey and please God. He reassures and confirms to our spirit that we are Born Again and redeemed by the Blood of Jesus Christ, the Messiah, the Anointed One. He also places our hand upon the heart of God so that we can experience His heartbeat---the Eternal Life flowing outward to all eternity: For God is Love.

CHAPTER TWO:

The Yoke Shall Be Destroyed!

27 "And it shall come to pass in that day, that his [Satan's] burden shall be taken away from off thy shoulders, and his yoke from off thy [our] neck, and the yoke shall be destroyed because of the anointing. 19 When the enemy [Satan] shall come in, like a flood the spirit of the Lord shall lift up a standard against him" Isa. 10.27; 59.19 (KJV).

Adam was entrusted with the Word of God. The Word of God was every word that proceeded out of His mouth. Among these words were commands that Adam "be fruitful and multiply and replenish the earth, and subdue it; and have dominion..." (Genesis 1:28). Thus because of the Word of God, Adam reigned as god of this world. Since it was the results of God's Word that Adam was given dominion and authority, it was also the disobeying of God's Word that ultimately caused Adam to lose his dominion and authority.

The modus operandi of the Word hasn't changed. Therefore, it's **our faith** in God's Word that maintains an activation of His Word in our lives. The **faith of god** is inherited in His Word. Our faith must unite with the Faith inherited in the Word to bring it to pass in our lives. In short, we must **agree with the word of God**.

18 "[For Abraham, human reason for] hope being gone, hoped IN FAITH that he should become the father of many nations, as he had been PROMISED, So [numberless] shall your descendants be" Ro. 4.18-21 (Amp. Bible).

"Human reason" often defies and defiles our Faith in the Word of God. The life of Abraham was not a life without temptations and controversy. His story wasn't recorded in the Holy Bible because he was perfect, a faultless example, or even that he fathered a child when he was "as good as dead" because of his age. Abraham wasn't known for the fact that Sarah's womb was barren, and the miracle that God performed in restoring her womb; and her natural beauty was such that King Abimelech---whom could have had his pick of the younger women---was dazzled and wanted her, though she was actually a senior citizen!

And though Abraham was twice struck down by a spirit of fear concerning his personal safety when traveling with Sarah, and he lied to King Abimelech, Abraham was known for his faith in God. Abraham, for the most part, believed that God was able to keep His promises. He considered not his natural ability, his physical appearance, wealth, community ties or what other people believed, but considered Him who would do exceeding and abundantly above all he could ask or think.

"Abraham believed God and it was counted unto him for righteousness" (Romans 4:3). Abraham believed in Him who justifies the ungodly (Romans 4:5). Abraham wasn't perfect but served a perfect God, who justified him by his faith, not works, and counted his faith as righteousness (Romans 4:22). "Therefore being justified by faith, we have peace with God through our Lord Jesus Christ" (Romans 4:25).

The peace we enjoy was purchased at the cross. Salvation, Sanctification, Healing and Deliverance was purchased by the Blood of Jesus Christ. It's by faith that we appropriate the dominion Christ won for us. As only by faith Adam, Abraham, the prophets and Jesus could please God, the Way has not changed. The Spiritual Laws do not apply to some people and not others.

"But without faith it is IMPOSSIBLE to please him; for he that cometh to God must BELIEVE that He is, and that He is a rewarder of them that diligently seek Him" (Hebrews 11:6).

We must first believe in the promises of God and that He will keep His promises. These are the two immutable concepts: God has made promises and God cannot lie.

The yoke-destroying power of the Anointing will drive out the Enemy. Like a flood, the Spirit of the Lord will lift up the heavenly standard of righteousness and bring about peace, healings and deliverances from the torments of demonic oppressions. His promises are available to whosoever will ask in Jesus' Name. When the Enemy comes in he comes to stay. It's not a visit but an occupation; it's not to steal our television, jewelry or sports car---but our health, soul and spirit.

He came to steal, kill and destroy everything of eternal weight in glory. The peace and tranquility of undisturbed rest and love is his target. "He **delivers** and **rescues,** and works signs and wonders in the heaven and in the earth, who hath delivered Daniel from the power of the lions" (Daniel 6:27). Daniel was delivered from the bone-crushing jaws of the hungry lions. His destruction was imminent; the plan was presumed flawless.

But the Enemy didn't take into account Daniel's faith in God. He was a man who knew the worth of prayer. Daniels faith transcended the physical realm and threat of danger, and delivered him from the power of the evil spirits using the satraps who got Daniel into the lion's den.

The schemes of the ruling spirits manipulated King Darius and his satraps. But God delivered Daniel from the obvious danger and the invisible attack. In fact, it was King Darius who praised God for Daniel's miraculous deliverance! The king realized the error of his ways—how he allowed people and his gods (who were actually evil spirits pretending to be God) manipulate him into doing evil. He came to believe in Daniel's God.

He proclaimed in faith: "He **delivers** and **rescues**". The Enemy came in but was swept away by the life-changing flood of the Spirit of God. The Prophet Joel wrote: "And it shall come to pass, that whosoever shall call upon the name of the Lord shall be **delivered** (Joel 2:32). while the apostle Paul wrote: "for whosoever shall call upon the name of the lord shall be **saved**" (Romans 10:13).

We discover that Deliverance was available before Salvation was; yet Salvation, the New Birth includes the provisions of Deliverance; and yet both are the Ministry of the Holy Spirit. In Christ we deal with Satan in a different way than the Old Testament. Jesus proclaimed in the synagogue, "The Spirit of the Lord is upon Me, because He hath **anointed me** to preach the gospel to the poor; He hath sent Me to heal the brokenhearted, to preach **deliverance** to the captives, and recovering of sight to the blind, to set at liberty them that are bruised, to preach the acceptable year of the Lord" (Lk. 4.18,19). It was the Spirit of the Lord, the Holy Spirit that was upon the man named Jesus of Nazareth.

The Spirit, the Anointing empowered Jesus to preach and do the Father's will. The Christ within Jesus, the Kingdom of God, cast out and eradicated everything contrary to His nature; bondages, sicknesses, diseases, poverty and death were challenged by Jesus and He claimed the victory over them. It was not who He was as a human being that made the difference. Certainly, it was the Anointing that brought the victory, the Presence of the Kingdom of God upon the scene.

"When the evening was come, they brought unto Him many that were possessed with devils: and he cast out the spirits with His word, and healed all that were sick: That it might be fulfilled which was spoken by Esaias (Isaiah) the prophet, saying, **Himself took our infirmities, and bare our sicknesses**" (Mt. 8.16, 17).

The scriptures point out that the deliverance work of the Lord was foretold centuries earlier. He fulfilled the will of God by Himself taking our infirmities, sicknesses and diseases. Yet that wasn't the end of the prophesies: "Himself" doesn't only mean Jesus of Nazareth ministering on earth for three years, but ministering FOREVER as the Christ, the Son of God. Therefore, when the Anointing is upon us it's the Lord Jesus Christ ministering---Himself casting out sicknesses and diseases.

Because the Anointing is Christ, we cannot accept any credit for the miracles performed through us. We humble ourselves and strive to become obedient unto death as was Jesus. As Abraham had no confidence in the flesh neither do we.

"And when He had called unto Him His twelve disciples, He gave them POWER AGAINST UNCLEAN SPIRITS, TO CAST THEM OUT, AND TO

HEAL ALL MANNER OF SICKNESS AND ALL MANNER OF DISEASES" (Matthew 10:1).

This was still HIMSELF working in the earth. The disciples were only His instruments. The power they received was the Holy Spirit; it was delegated authority to minister under the same covenant Jesus ministered under. God cannot and will not interfere in our lives without our permission; and God has done all He's going to do concerning these spirits-- He triumphed over them by the cross. "That through death [and the resurrection that followed] He might destroy him that had the power over death, that is, the Devil" (He. 2.14).

He abolished the Devil's authority over the children of God (the unsaved are still in the Devil's family.), and the sting of death. He gave the Church authority to heal and cast out demons. What a remarkable Lord! The Prayer of Agreement was another secret that Jesus revealed. "If two of you shall agree..." will manifest the Third, HIMSELF, bringing to bear the corporate Anointing that is upon the entire Church.

The Armor Of God

10 "...be strong in the Lord and the power of His might. 11 Put on the whole armor of God, that ye may be able to stand against the wiles of the Devil. 14...girt about with Truth...Breastplate of Righteousness 15...feet Shod with the Preparation of the Gospel of Peace. 16...Shield of Faith.17...Helmet of Salvation, and the Sword of the Spirit, which is the Word of God" Eph. 6.10,11,14-17.

Though we're seated In Him, in the Third Heaven, and at the Throne of God, our Soul and Physical Bodies live within the realms of demonic activity; our self-life and consciousness is an assignment for demon spirits. When we were Born Again and positioned with Christ, we were granted access to the body armor of the saints of God. We can-- and must---put on the armor of God and then stand against the schemes of the unclean devils on the ground and in the atmosphere around us.

The **Belt of Truth** fights the lies and deceptions of Satan. He wants us to think that he has more authority than Jehovah-Elohim or Christians. Satan wants us to believe that he maintains complete control of the world, and the destinies of the 6.7 billion people who live on Earth. Only the Word of God, the Truth can make us free.

The **Breastplate of Righteousness** is God's approval, His Justifying us by Faith in Jesus Christ, the Messiah. Satan attacks our mind, our emotions and tells us we'll always be sinners--snarling pitiful creatures. But the Word states that we're the righteousness of God In Christ Jesus. God loves and approves of us; God sees us as the Children of the Resurrection. We're In Him and He's in us. We are loved, accepted and blessed with all spiritual blessings.

The **Shoes** represent our being prepared by the Holy Spirit to be used in His Ministry; it's our submission to the Divine Purpose, our willingness to do good works, to produce good fruit, that Jehovah-Elohim will receive glory. We're saved by Grace through Faith--yet to advance and buildup the Kingdom of God on Earth we witness, testify, teach and preach the Word of Faith. We minister through Agape Love, Healing and Deliverance to all peoples, across denominations, racial and economic lines.

The Anointing on the feet, and the armor of the **Shoes** quenches the fiery darts of Satan who wants us to believe that witnessing to the lost is a waste of time and money. Satan whispers that there are too many countries, people, languages and dialects to successfully reach the 6.7 Billion people; he says that there are insurmountable racial, cultural, political and religious barriers--obstacles he has placed there--and not enough committed workers, financial resources to purchase food, medicine and personal needs to reach the hardest hit areas on the planet. But Satan is a liar! The Anointing on the feet and the armor of the Shoes defeats Satan.

The **Shield of Faith** protects us from demonic attacks through the invisible realm against our mind and body. The Shield of Faith protects us from mental, emotional and physical attacks, insults, temptations and hindrances to our prayer and Calling. We believe, have Faith in the Word of God, trust in and rely on God's promises. We therefore enforce the New Testament Covenant with zeal, an available and humble spirit of devotion. Often the Spiritual Gift of Faith, the Faith of God manifests as He adds to our faith, His Faith, to reinforce our shielding during the heaviest of satanic attacks. The command to **stand** resides in us.

The **Helmet** of **Salvation**: Salvation is the area of Satan's first strike. If he failed to stop us from getting Saved, his next move is to persuade us to doubt our Salvation, or to enter into the trap of unbelief concerning the Word of God. Satan wants us to doubt the greatness of Jesus Christ, His Name, His Blood and His victory at Calvary. Satan wants us to doubt God's ability to keep His promises and perform His Word as written in the Holy Bible. Satan wants us to doubt our position In Him and at His Throne in the Third Heaven; to believe that the promises and Anointing of God was only for the Jewish prophets and leaders of ancient Israel, the Old Testament days and the early church history. Satan wants to rob us of the Blessing. He doesn't want us to experience the Faith and joy of our Salvation. But the Anointing of God, the Helmet of Salvation bulldozes through the dung heap of Satan's crappy schemes; Satan has no wind to run this race with us!

The **Sword of the Spirit** is the Word of God. Jesus said, "It is written..." The Word of God rising from our heart and spoken out of our mouth sends Satan and his troops fleeing for parts unknown. We being rooted and grounded in the Word provides us with a mammoth-size sword to strike down the oppression, obsession, depression and possession by unclean spirits. We pray and stand our ground, waiting patiently for the Word of God to manifest, the Sword of the Spirit to fall. If doubt or any such deception comes we slice it with our Sword. We can't afford to let the Word of God depart from before our eyes, for He has magnified His Word above all His Name. We as doers of the Word and not hears only overcome the world.

Spiritual Warfare

4 "The weapons we fight with are not weapons of the world. ...they have divine power to **demolish strongholds**" 2 Cor. 10. (NIV).

The strongholds that Paul wrote about aren't the Second Heaven Demonic Government; we're not to be overly concerned but aware of its existence and influence. The strongholds we're concerned with exist in our mind. The thoughts, feelings, emotions and imaginations---the desires of the flesh, eyes, and the pride of the self-life and conformity to the world system---are the strongholds to be taken captive and brought down by obedience to the Word of God.

"And be not conformed to this world: but be ye **transformed** by the **renewing of your mind**..." (Ro. 12:2). Face it, we have issues to work on. These issues are predominately from the past, brought into the present by our mental functions of memory and emotions; or tormenting spirits use our negative history in the present to manipulate, intimidate and dominate us, through our thought-stream; these thoughts and feelings have a powerful effect on our present thoughts and behaviors.

These strongholds, attitudes, prejudices, codes, beliefs that we've lived by as an un-regenerated sinner, are presently affecting our relationship with Jesus and His Body. Nevertheless, through the unsearchable riches of Jesus Christ, has He conferred upon His heirs an arsenal of spiritual weaponry. These weapon systems intercept and cancel the works of Satan and the works **of** the flesh. We wield the nine **Fruit of the Spirit** to assist us: **Love, Joy, Peace, Patience, Kindness, Goodness, Faithfulness, Meekness and Self-Control** (Gal. 5.22,23).

The second order of spiritual weapons, the **Spiritual Gifts** are: **Tongues, Interpretation of Tongues, Gifts of Healing, Prophecy, Word of Wisdom, Word of Knowledge, Discerning of Spirits, Faith and Working of Miracles** (1 Cor. 12.8-11).

These gifts also detect and monitor the demonic activity around us. From our position in the Third Heaven we can know in advance what Satan has planned, even his "local" maneuvers and operations. Through the Spiritual Gifts we crush Satan's resistance to the New Testament Covenant, his attacks upon us in defiance to God's authority, and who we are In Christ. Together these eighteen weapons and "radar" systems help us get the victory over our mind, the world, and the evil spirits. Jesus Christ gave us government within His Body that occupies the Earth; the field offices are the **Five-Fold Ministry: Apostles, Prophets, Evangelists, Pastors, Teachers** (Eph. 4:11).

We Believers receive instructions through our official leaders. Jesus Christ is our Commander-in-Chief; these leaders are likened to generals. None of the weapons of our warfare are conventional, nuclear, biological or chemical---but they can utterly loose the bonds of wickedness and undue every yoke! Our "It is written..." attitude in prayer and speech must replace the old unprofitable "begging" God to do what He has already empowered us to do by Faith; or seeking Deliverance from the mental health sciences or demon-inspired groups, when the problem is that we're too lazy to study, believe and practice the Word of God, thus our mind isn't significantly renewed. Desires of the flesh can't be exorcised---cast off the bone; only demon spirits can be cast out. The Medical Sciences has met their limitation when demon spirits are involved. They can treat the ailments of the flesh and perhaps a physically damaged brain, and drug us senseless or unconscious, but cannot get to the root cause if that cause is demon infestation.

19 "The acts of the sinful nature (the works of the flesh) are obvious: sexual immorality, impurity and debauchery, 20 idolatry and witchcraft; hatred, discord, jealousy, fits of rage, selfish ambition, dissensions, factions, 21 and envy; drunkenness, orgies, and the like"--- Galatians 5.19-21 (NIV).

The inference of this scripture is upon **we** as a Christian to crucify the fleshly desires, not storming the demonic realms or praying down the Spiritual Wickedness in the heavens---but accepting responsibility, accountability and obtaining control of our mental thoughts, emotions, feelings and actions. We have to **work out our own Salvation**, renewing of our mind, as a partner with the Holy Spirit. He isn't going to do all the work and we can't do it without Him.

We don't want to indulge, go back to the old sinful "works of the flesh", so we have to be diligent. Relaxing and meditating on the Word can break the compulsive, neurotic or psychotic merry-go-round of repetitive sinful habits that we can't conquer by sheer will power. The Word has Deliverance and Healing power. "He sent His Word and healed them" (Ps. 107.20). Hindrance to our spiritual growth is our old ways standing in the way of our new ways. Unbelief and doubt opposes Faith.

Inner Healing and Deliverance

Luke 6:46 Jesus said, "Why do you call Me, Lord, Lord, and do not what I say?" There are a number of reasons why we do not obey the Lord as we desire to. Many of these reasons point to the need for Inner Healing and Deliverance. The character of our New Man, recreated in Christ Jesus, is being defiled by the "bitter root" character of our Old Man; the nature of our Old Man, as described in Hebrews 12:15, has not been fully taken to the cross of Christ to experience death, and is clandestinely plotting to overthrow the Lordship of Jesus Christ over us, Whose Holy Spirit resides in our human spirits. The Old Sin Nature desires to express itself through our self-life by sprouting roots of influence, in order to reclaim its leadership position.

Evangelizing Unbelieving Hearts

Hebrews 3:12 "take care, **brethren** (the church) lest there be in any one of you an evil, unbelieving heart, in falling away from the living God." Because the Old Man refuses to remain dead, deep in our hearts there remains some measure of unbelief. Inner Healing is actually evangelism, a ministry bringing the Gospel to those parts of our Believer's heart that have not yet believed and received Salvation. Romans 10:9 states that it is "belief in the heart" that brings Salvation: Much of what we have acquired of the Gospel is divided between "heart belief" and "head knowledge."

Many Christians cannot live the Gospel because we have believed only with the mind; our faith has not totally conquered our hearts. The Ministry of Inner Healing is to reach the hearts of born-again Christians with the good news of Salvation. V.10 "For with the heart man believes, resulting in righteousness, and with the mouth he confesses, resulting in salvation." So, the Ministry of Inner Healing is to evangelize the unbelieving hearts of Believers; it is the application of the blood, cross and resurrection life of our Lord Jesus Christ to those stubborn dimensions of our heart (including character flaws, strongholds, bondages and personality disorders) that have so far refused the redemption our mind and spirit requested when we invited Jesus in. Often this refusal is the presence or influence of unclean spirits in the soul or physical bodies; but, again, the Anointing destroys EVERY conceivable yoke.

Inner Healing and Sanctification

Salvation or Regeneration comes after we have repented, confessed our sins and by faith accepted Jesus Christ as our Lord and Savior, then we miraculously receive the indwelling of the Holy Spirit in our human spirits, which raises us from spiritual death to spiritual life. After that comes Sanctification, which is the lifelong process in which the Holy Spirit transforms our mind (Romans 12:2), character and personality to be exactly like Jesus.

The Ministry of Inner Healing is a tool of the Holy Spirit to effect changes in our individual lives. Inner Healing does not erase a memory or change our personal history. Rather it enables us to cherish even the worst moments in our lives, for through them God has inscribed eternal lessons onto our hearts and prepared us to minister to all who have suffered in the same way. In this, Romans 8:28 is clear; All things do work together for the good to those who love God and are called according to His purpose.

What is Inner Healing?

Inner healing is the healing of memories and emotions, the taking to the cross of Christ the self, that it may experience death, the application of the crucified and resurrected Life of Jesus Christ; it is also prayer, biblical counseling to effect mental and spiritual stability, Sanctification, consecration which leads to Transformation. The difference between Psychology and Inner Healing is that Inner Healing is based on the Word of God; the Christian is to die to the self-life, self-will, self-oriented goals and motivations that are outside of God's will and purpose for our life.

Psychology seeks to restore our self-image, an image given to us by the world system of standards; this philosophy is based on the theory that if we see ourselves as adequate, competent and good, we will have great self-esteem, the confidence to conform to the expectations of a Christ-less society and perform well: it is like creating a sinner who thinks well of himself, a new and improved sinner.

Seven Steps to Inner Healing & Deliverance

1. Renunciation
2. Forgiveness
3. Humility
4. Prayer
5. Repentance
6. Warfare
7. Faith

Four Levels of Demonic Activity in Humans

First Level Infestation: Demonic spirit have gathered about a person but not inside of him. Example: Blocking Spirits and Familiar Spirits.

Second Level: Inhabitation: Demonic spirit has entered but has been limited by the Holy Spirit.

Third Level: Obsession: Inhabiting Demon has come out of hiding to assume control of character structure. In Unbelievers and Nominal Christians demon can live within the inmost self and control psychologically Spirit-Filled Christians, through negative or sinful emotions, fantasies, hidden motives, behaviors and attitudes in the members.

Fourth Level: Possession or Ownership, original personality entirely suppressed. Christians cannot be possessed.

Spiritual Principles

1. Demons cannot read our mind.
2. Demons attack Saved and Unsaved people.

3. Inner Healing isn't confessing old sins.
4. Everything bad that happens to us isn't demonic.
5. Demons must be invited in before they can occupy.
6. All Christians have the authority to cast out demons.
7. Demons can attack through another person.
8. Demons can talk through the mouth of people.
9. Demons can communicate thoughts and ideas or talk to the mind of a person without the person being conscious or aware of it.
10. Deliverance Ministers are protected by the Holy Spirit from demons attempting to transfer from client to them.
11. Deliverance is exorcism, the casting out of demons.
12. Sickness and Disease is often due to demons in the soul or physical bodies.

Adamic Sin, Generational Sin, Curses, Disobedience and sinful lifestyle gives demons a legal right to torment and inhabit. Demons are fallen angels and cannot be Saved. Satan is the prince of the demonic kingdom.

Laying On of Hands

17 "And these signs shall follow them that believe: In My Name they shall cast out devils...18 ...they shall lay hands on the sick, and they shall recover"---Mk. 16.17,18 (KJV).

The **Doctrine of the Laying on of Hands** has become a controversial topic in the latter day reign of the Church. According to Jesus, the Apostles and the Believers of the early Church, the Laying on of Hands was a part of the exercise of faith in the Lord Jesus, and there were plenty of miracles.

Jesus commanded (not suggested) "all" His disciples to cast out devils and lay hands on the sick, as demonstrating the delegated authority that He gave us. He also said that certain signs shall follow the Believer. The ordinations, presbyteries, missionary journeys and healing services were energized by the Laying on of Hands.

The "fear merchants"---those who quickly point out a dreadful consequence to a true scriptural action---in order to satisfy their carnal or religious beliefs, interpret as doctrines their own opinions as holy scripture. The merchants make logical arguments and excuses to condone their failure to obey the Lord's Commandment regarding exorcising demons and healing the sick. So today the traditional, denominational pastors just want to preach to a well-dressed audience, pick up their check and go home.

To justify their religious doctrines, with Satan's guidance, thousands of pastors shout "BEWARE" OF SATAN!" to their Church members who want to obey Jesus by laying hands on demonized or diseased persons; they are cautioned that demons or sicknesses would transfer to the Christian or their families.

They quote 1 Timothy 5:22 which states, "Lay hands on no man suddenly," which isn't a reference to demons or sickness, but Paul was advising Timothy against appointing Church leaders who were new Christians, whose character was questionable or not known. Hands were laid on Church leaders when they were installed in office! Today many Church leaders misuse the above scripture and in so doing imply that Satan has more power than God; then young Christians wonder why so many pastors are forced or leave their pulpits because gross sin was discovered in their lives.

These pastors needed Deliverance but were too proud or ignorant to ask for help. Many Church leaders stand behind their "safe" philosophy when dealing with something they know little or nothing about: Deliverance. They lack information and the determined purpose to seek out the whole truth; they lack faith to believe in the **progressive work of the Holy Spirit, called Sanctification.**

To them, everything stopped at the cross, a finished work; that is, the opportunity to go to Heaven after death is all we received from His Finished Work! Then, why is there so much sinning in the Body of Christ? How is it that we need a crowbar to pry a Pastor's hand off the arm of a slot machine--- or both hands from around his wife's neck?! These days, it's not unusual to hear on the local news of crimes committed by men and women in ministry authority.

Pastors who lack adequate faith in Deliverance and Healing teach the congregation of the dreadful consequences in stepping out of the boat; they always tell the story of how Peter's lack of faith caused him to sink, but not the fact that he got out the boat, walked on the water, while the other eleven watched safely from the boat; at least Peter got out the boat! He did his best to obey Jesus who said to him, "Come." Old wives tales, worn-out traditions and scare tactics---all of which are satanic in origin, has made the Word of God of no effect in the lives of many Christians.

We cannot get victory over sickness, disease or demons because we are afraid to let another Christian anoint and lay hands on us! Know that by faith we are protected by the Spirit of God to receive help and to give our help; we are protected by the Blood of Jesus, and cannot be "compromised" by unclean spirits while in the performance of our Christian duties. The spirit of fear is the reason why a lot of us are without spiritual strength, or having great difficulty in fulfilling our destinies. But hold on. help is on the way. We must say out loud: It is for freedom that Christ has set me free!   Let us not be like King Saul, who in his last days came to this conclusion: "I have played the fool, and have erred exceedingly!"--- 1 Sam. 26.21.

An Awesome Spirit Being

A yoke is a wooden harness that fastens two beasts together; the farmer attaches two animals of the same size and strength, so they will pull equally, and thus the furrows would be straight. However, in spiritual terms, Satan the strong Beast yoked to us as weak, un-Saved or a carnal Christian, he would dominate and take us where he wants to go. So is the case with many people. But the Yoke is destroyed by **The Anointed One and His Anointing!**

The Mystery of Christ is so deep. When we consider that Jesus was both God and man, the Son of God and the Son of Man, an attempt to separate the two for the sake of understanding, we discover a paradox, and that too is a mystery. It is assumed---for lack of a better word---that Jesus of Nazareth had a human spirit, human soul, and human body. This would be necessary to be totally human; but He also had Christ the Word resident within Him, most likely in His human spirit. Jesus is an awesome Spirit Being. Yet, Jesus said the reason why He could do such miracles was not because He's God, but that He was Anointed by the Holy Spirit to do them.

Before His baptism in the Holy Spirit, Jesus of Nazareth, a man predestined to be the Lord, had the potential of being our Savior, but could choose not to sacrifice Himself, and thereby disobey God and become like the rest of us---sinners. Of Course the Holy Spirit within Jesus of Nazareth was already the Lord God, but His soul, mind and physical body had to be changed into the image of God. Jesus had personality shaped from His parents.

God also gave Him revelation, and used Jesus' environment and social relationships to teach Him obedience. He had individuality and opinions, which He chose not to exalt. Instead, He exalted the will of the Father: He would become the Lamb of God. This shouldn't surprise us, seeing we're His spiritual descendents; we're earthen vessels indwelled by the Holy Spirit. This alone gives us the potential to do great and mighty works for the Kingdom of God. We too are **awesome spirit beings with infinite potential**. And this was the purpose of His incarnation: To raise up the names of the (spiritually)dead, our names, upon our inheritance. He came to raise all the Lazarus' that desired to be raised from the dead. In the Physical Realm, binding and loosing authority was conferred upon the Church, the children of God. The authority and Spirit power to put demons and their works to flight is in our Covenant. Whatever God doesn't permit in Heaven because it's improper and unlawful, we don't have to allow on earth either! Even the Spiritual Wickedness, the princes who rule the lower heavens are made ineffective by Christ, in response to our prayers and Christian authority to administer the New Testament Covenant.

It's the Physical Realm where the binding and loosing is first initiated, not in Heaven. It's in the Physical Realm where the Church must come into unity---agreement, harmony, a symphony-- with the Church at the throne of God. The Physical Body of Christ must agree with the Spiritual Body of Christ in Heaven, before the Holy Spirit will change things down here; it's God's will. This is where we as Christians miss the mark: We spend a lot of time not praying---but begging for God to do what He already gave us authority to do. When the Church was an infant and needed a lot of help, He was there to carry her; now the Church is over two thousand years old, she should be walking with Him. The Church should be strong and ruling the world; but the world is ruling the Church---binding and loosing us!

He said, "Behold, I give you power to tread on serpents and scorpions, and over ALL THE POWER OF THE ENEMY; and nothing shall by any means hurt you" (Luke 9:19). These are the signs that follow them that believe; these aren't just signs for the Ministry Gifts: Apostles, prophets, evangelists, pastors, or teachers---but signs and wonders that follow ANY believer in Christ Jesus.

True, the Ministry Gifts have received delegated leadership anointing and a greater measure of the Holy Spirit; but all Believers, some more than others are anointed by the Holy Spirit. The Holy Spirit flows through Christ's Body, bringing it into unity with Himself. The Word of God, Name of Jesus, and Blood of Jesus are integrated into the Covenant of Blessing. Seeing we have in us the consummation of the Covenant, Christ in us, and have submitted to God, resisting the Devil can, with great pleasure, say, spirit of sickness---in the Name of Jesus---leave! Jesus stated as Believers in Him we have the same authority on earth as we have in Heaven. The key to victory is knowing and putting into practice the scriptures, knowing Whose and who we are. Our very words have Spirit power when faith is added to them. We must "say" to the mountains in our life--be thou removed! These mountains may be sickness, poverty, depression or oppression of the Devil; they may be addictions, fears, or marital problems; they could even be everyday stress from working and raising a family.

Whenever the Holy Spirit is needed, we can speak Him into our situation. We can also run demons out of our life or the lives of those we pray for. By speaking the Word of Faith, we confer blessings to come upon and overtake those we pray for. But the enemy of faith is doubt. We must not doubt in our heart that God is ready, willing and able to meet our needs. In short, we must have FAITH IN GOD AND THE FAITH OF GOD.

God has great faith because He is the Father of faith. God believes---adheres to, trust in, and relies on---His words; we must also apply this biblical definition and believe in our own Spirit-inspired words in order to manifest them; As awesome spirit beings God has given us exceedingly great and precious promises. When Jesus walked the earth as the Son of man, He performed thousands of healings, miracles, signs and wonders.

At great length He described the provisions, guarantees and oaths of the New Testament Covenant. He graciously spoke to the crowd about the Promise of the Father, that He would return to the Father. He was the kernel of wheat that would fall to the earth and die. But when He did, He would send back the Comforter to forever abide with His followers.

"For John truly baptized with water; but **YOU SHALL BE BAPTIZED WITH THE HOLY GHOST** not many days hence" Then He continued and said, "But **YOU SHALL RECEIVE POWER**, after that the Holy Ghost is come upon you; and you shall be witnesses unto Me..." (Acts 1:5,B).

When the Lord Jesus Christ arose from the dead, He ascended into Heaven with the captives of Sheol. From the throne of God He sent back to the Physical Realm the Promise of the Father which is the Holy Spirit. With the arrival of the Holy Spirit came the authority and endowment of power for all Believers to become like Christ. The **Resurrection Anointing** to destroy yokes was now surging through the Body of Christ in the Physical Realm.

The Church was first established at the throne of God, then on the day of Pentecost, it was established in the Physical Realm. Jesus also sent back the **Leadership Anointing**, the **Ministry Gifts**: "And He gave some, **apostles**; some, **prophets**; and some, **evangelist**; and some, **pastors**; and some, **teachers; For the perfecting of the saints**, for the **work of the ministry**, for the **edifying of the body of Christ: Till we all come in the unity of the faith**, and of the knowledge of the Son of God, unto a perfect (complete) man, unto the measure of the statue of the fullness of Christ" (Eph. 4.11-13).

Not only did God anoint Jesus Christ with the Holy Ghost and with power, but Jesus Christ became the One who Baptizes us in the Holy Spirit! He has placed in the Church anointed people to channel His Blessing into the congregation. He did this to exhort, instruct, correct, rebuke, and expose the hidden wisdom and knowledge in the heart of God; even the hidden mysteries and treasures not obvious to the natural mind, are daily being revealed to those who possess the Ministry Gifts.

The Holy Spirit is given through grace---unmerited favor; Salvation is received in response to repentance of sins and confession of faith in Jesus Christ. The authority and privilege to be called children of God is based upon voluntarily receiving the Holy Spirit; the Baptism in the Holy Spirit, the second work of grace, is also received by faith. The Holy Spirit, a living Person walks among us seeking those who have been called and predestined to Salvation.

He woos us to freely accept Jesus so He can enter our spirit and make His residence there. Because the Holy Spirit is God, He has the authority to forgive sins and to save. The ability to make confession of sins and confession of faith in Jesus Christ comes from the wooing in our heart by the Holy Spirit. He brings us to repentance. Without the Holy Spirit to strengthen us, we cannot live what we confess with our mouth. Though we may sincerely believe what we have decided in our heart, we cannot perform or live the Christian lifestyle without the help of the Holy Spirit. Through this, we become **awesome spirit beings with infinite potential**.

"Then Samuel took the horn of oil, and anointed him in the midst of his brethren, "and the Spirit of the Lord came upon David from that day forward" (1 Sam.16:13). David became one of several awesome spirit beings in the Old Testament. In the above verse, he was anointed king of Israel. God's decision to anoint David king wasn't based on who David was, but God looked upon David's humble respect and disposition towards His Name.

Then God anointed David to be captain over His inheritance, and a **new creation, a man after God's own heart**. Though David was anointed and loved God, he wasn't sinless; he made plenty of mistakes; for all have sinned and missed the mark. Moreover, David had a personal relationship with God. David claimed his Covenant right and cleaved to it with his very life; God in return claimed His Covenant right, and wouldn't leave David or forsake him.

David was a type of Christ; he was anointed by the Holy Spirit as king of Israel. David was also a priest of a different order and rank than the Levitical Order. Therefore, David had the authority to confer blessings upon the people, as being a priest of a new order of king-priest, having been approved by God. David was a chosen vessel, an example of how God can change an ordinary man into an extraordinary man. Though David was a skillful warrior and wise king, the praise and glory belongs to the Lord, who Covenanted with him, conformed and transformed David from a shy shepherd boy into a type of Christ.

It is God who causes us to triumph. He seats us in heavenly places with Himself. We're saved by grace through faith in Him. We're justified, sanctified and partakers of His divine nature. Having been redeemed from the curse of the Mosaic Law, and delivered from the powers of darkness, we're led by the Spirit of the Son.

"And from Jesus Christ, who is the faithful witness, and the first begotten of the dead, and the Prince of the kings of the earth. Unto Him that loved us, and washed us from our sins in His own blood. And bath **MADE US KINGS AND PRIESTS UNTO GOD** and His Father; to Him be glory and dominion forever and ever. Amen" (Revelation 1:6). God said it; all we need to do is believe it. John wrote of the blessed, the redeemed of the Lord. All our needs are met by and through Jesus Christ. He's our High Priest, the Mediator between God and Man. One day when the trials and tribulations in the physical are over, we'll sing a new song; it's a song that the heavenly angels can't sing--because they weren't redeemed by the Blood of Jesus.

"And they sung a new song, saying, Thou art worthy to take the book, and to open the seals thereof: for Thou was slain, and hast redeemed us to

God by Thy blood out of every kindred, and tongue, and people, and nation; And hast **MADE US UNTO GOD KINGS AND PRIESTS**; and we shall reign on the earth" (Rev. 5.9,10).

We're kings and priests. Kings must have kingdoms, priests must have ministries: We reign and govern with Him in the Physical Realm, New Jerusalem, and in Heaven. If we're to be good leaders and ministers in Heaven, we need to start be the same here, practicing conformity to the example of Christ. This Physical Realm is God's classroom. As the righteousness of God in Christ, we must submit to the Holy Spirit and become an imitator.

"Blessed and holy is he that hath part in the first resurrection: on such the second death hath no power, but they shall be **PRIESTS OF GOD AND OF CHRIST**, and shall reign with Him a thousand years" (Rev. 20:6).

The yoke shall be destroyed because of the Anointing, and we become awesome spirit beings!

CHAPTER THREE

Spiritual Gifts:

In Acts Chapter Two is recorded the events of the Day of Pentecost, the birth of the Earthbound Church. On that day the Holy Spirit arrived to empower Believers not only to establish the foundation doctrines and material buildings of the Church, but the **Spiritual Essence of Divine Church** throughout the generations to come. However, for centuries the Divine Essence has been replaced by religion, legalism, formalism and materialism.

Few seek to acquire Spiritual Gifts but only monetary gifts---and this includes Church Leaders. This booklet is for those who seek the Kingdom and its Righteousness, and Spiritual Gifts to adequately serve the King of Kings and Lord of Lords.

"Now about Spiritual Gifts (special endowments of supernatural energy), brethren, I do not want you to be misinformed.

4 Now there are distinctive varieties and distributions of endowments (gifts, extraordinary powers distinguishing certain Christians, due to the power of divine Grace operating in their souls by the Holy Spirit) and they vary, but the [Holy] Spirit remains the same.

5 And there are distinctive varieties of service and ministration, but it is the same Lord [Who is served].

6 And there are distinctive varieties of operation [of working to accomplish things], but it is the same God Who inspires and energizes them all in all.

7 But to each one is given the manifestation of the [Holy] Spirit [the evidence, the spiritual illumination of the Spirit] for good and profit.

8 To one is given in and through the [Holy] Spirit [the power to speak] a message, or **Word of Wisdom**, and to another [the power to express] a **Word of Knowledge** and understanding according to the same [Holy] Spirit;

9 To another [wonder-working] **Faith** by the same [Holy] Spirit, to another the extraordinary powers or **Gifts of Healing** by the same Spirit.

10 To another the **Working of Miracles**, to another **Prophecy**, prophetic insight (the gift of interpreting the divine will and purpose); to another the ability to **Discern Spirits** and distinguish between [the utterances of true] spirits [and false ones], to another various kinds of [unknown] **Tongues**, to another the ability to **Interpret** [such] tongues.

11 All these [gifts, achievements, abilities] are inspired and brought to pass by one and the same [Holy] Spirit, Who apportions to each person individually [exactly] as He chooses ---1 Cor. 12.1,4-11 (Amp. Bible).

Three Groups of Three
Gifts of Revelations: Word of Wisdom, Word of Knowledge, Discerning of Spirits.
Gifts of Power: Faith, Working of Miracles, Gifts of Healing.
Gifts of Inspiration: Prophecy, Tongues, Interpretation of Tongues.

Word of Wisdom

The Word of Wisdom is the first of the three Gifts of Revelation.

Definition: The Word of Wisdom can be defined as a supernatural revelation of the mind and purpose of God communicated by the Holy Spirit. It's God's wisdom imparted to us; designated as the gift of the Word of God's wisdom. When the Lord specifically reveals His purpose to us, we possess a word of God's wisdom.

However, this gift should not be confused with the daily guidance of the Holy Spirit, the practical wisdom obtained to live by and to make wise decisions. Practical wisdom and the Word of Wisdom are not the same; practical wisdom may come through life experiences or by reading the Holy Bible. Because the Revelation Gifts are similar, Christians often confuse the Word of Wisdom with the simple gift of Prophecy. Prophecy is NOT fortunetelling. The term "prophecy" is often used generally to describe the Word of Wisdom in operation. The Word of Wisdom (**wisdom-knowledge of the future**) or Word of Knowledge (**knowledge of the present or past**) is usually heard in a prophetic utterance. At times, more than one Revelation Gift may be present in a prophetic message.

We should listen carefully to distinguish between the different gifts.

Example: A glass of tea (a prophetic message) can contain sugar (Word of Knowledge) and milk (Word of Wisdom) yet is still considered tea (a prophetic message).

How the Word of Wisdom may come to us: By an angel, like Gideon at the winepress; In a vision, as Daniel received revelations; in dreams, as Joseph received; an audible voice, as Moses heard God speaking from the burning bush. There is nothing greater than the revelation of the mind and purpose of God. The Word of Wisdom transports us to the very council chambers of God---His heart---and affords us a participation, however infinitesimal, in the government of the universe.

Since the Lord God will do nothing until He reveals it to His servants the Prophets. God wants His people "informed". He will not have us ignorant of His goings forth in Heaven and Earth.

Word of Knowledge

The Word of Knowledge is the companion gift to the Word of Wisdom. In a sense it is more like the Word of Wisdom than any other gift; but as wisdom and knowledge differ, so the Word of Wisdom and the Word of Knowledge differ. The Word of Know-ledge pertains to the past or present events of Heaven and the Physical Realm. The Word of Knowledge has NOTHING to do with human intelligence, IQ, knowledge gained through Bible College or personal study (for knowledge of the Word IS NOT the Word of Knowledge), natural talents, memorization, but is strictly supernatural.

Definition: The Word of Knowledge is a supernatural revelation of the existence or nature of a person, place or thing, or the **past or present** knowledge of some place or event, given to us by the Holy Spirit for a specific purpose. All the gifts produce signs and wonders that will attract or strengthen the faith of many Christians and non-Christians alike. The Word of Knowledge is also a participation to some infinitesimal degree in the **Omniscience** (all knowingness) of God. If the Lord who knows all things is pleased to reveal to us by His Spirit any fragment of His unlimited knowledge, then we can claim to have this manifestation of the Holy Spirit which is designated the Word of Knowledge.

Examples: The Word of Knowledge is a sign: It left Nathanael amazed when the Lord Jesus said to him, "Before that Phillip called you, when you were under the fig tree, I saw you" (Jn. 1.48). The Word of Knowledge can also direct us to locate a person who is lost, as in the instance of King Saul who hid himself from Samuel who came to anoint him king of Israel.

Or, the gift used as when Ananias was told to meet the converted Saul of Tarsus who was praying in a house on a street called "Straight" (Acts 9.11). Or the gift might expose some secret sins like the woman at the well in Samaria who had several husbands (Jn. 4.17-19). To be the Word of Knowledge it must be super-natural guidance. A word of caution needs to be interjected here: Being in possession of Spiritual Gifts isn't a sign of Spiritual Maturity or even that God is remotely pleased with our behavior!

In the same manner that going to Church does not necessarily produce Spiritual Maturity, having Spiritual Gifts is no guarantee of good Christian Character. There is no automatic transference between the **Fruit of the Spirit (character of God imparted)** and the **Gifts of the Spirit (power of God imparted)**, although the Holy Spirit administers both, and a holy lifestyle is the best foundation possible for spiritual manifestations.

Remember, the judges, prophets and apostles weren't perfect, devoid of character flaws, but had Spiritual Gifts. The gifts and callings of God are irrevocable. We are exhorted to covet earnestly the best gifts; and it's the prerogative of the Holy Spirit to divide them severally as He wills.

Discerning of Spirits

Discerning of Spirits is the last of the Gift of Revelation. This gift gives us an insight into the Spiritual World---the world beyond our natural eye sight. This gift is NOT a discerning of evil spirits only, but a **discerning of all spirits, good or evil, including the disposition, emotions, motives or intent of the heart of human beings.** It is the ability to see the presence or activity of a spirit through a revelation which God gives by the Holy Spirit.

All true visions which are of God (not demonic-inspired or nightmares) are manifestations of this gift. Therefore hallucinations, delusions, human desires, drugged or delirious minds are not included in this gift.

The Discerning of Spirits is a manifestation of the Holy Spirit, a vision given by God, and the Gift is unaided by the natural mind. If we could see into the Spirit realm, we would have greater insight into spiritual matters, and would be able to discern the powers, the causes which have prompted certain effects in the material world--- because this world is not what it seems to be: God, angels, Satan, demons and human spirits are operating in this world and beyond (many human beings daily astral project and soul travel).

Definition: The Discerning of Spirits is a gift of the Holy Spirit by which we are able to see into the Spirit Realm. By this insight we can discern the similitude of God, the risen Christ, the Holy spirit, cherubims, seraphims, archangels, hosts of angels, Satan and his legions. The Discerning of Spirits also will give us an insight into the disposition of persons: The presence of demon power possessing or oppressing a person.

An exception to this gift is concerning the ministry of angels on the earth who have been given material bodies; these angels can be seen by the natural eye and touched by anyone.

Examples: Jacob wrestled with an angel; if he saw the angel with his natural eyes it wasn't the gift of Discerning of Spirits. Abraham saw the Lord in human manifestation. The Lord Jesus was seen after His resurrection. But if an angel appeared in the midst of a crowd of people, only those with the gift of Discerning of Spirits activated at that moment would see the angel. Stephen before he was martyrdom saw the Lord Jesus sitting on the right hand of God---but no one else saw this. It was by this gift that Elisha comforted his servant when the hill was surrounded by the Syrian Army: Elisha prayed that God would open the servant's (spiritual) eyes. And when He did, the servant saw heavenly horses and chariots of fire.

Isaiah saw in a vision the Lord, "high and lifted up, and His train filled the temple" (Isa. 6.1). From Abraham to Paul who seen an angel, the gift of Discerning of Spirits has been recorded operating in human beings; and now it can operate in us too. To receive revelation or be enlightened about good or evil spirits without seeing them, is the manifestation of the Word of Wisdom or Word of Knowledge. One may discern an evil spirit within a person and not have the gift of Faith, or the know-how to cast it out.

Faith

The Gift of Faith is the first and greatest of the **Gifts of Power, the Omnipotence of God**. The Gift of Faith is NOT SIMPLE FAITH, the faith that saves the soul, nor is it the Fruit of the Spirit called Faithfulness. **Definition:** The Gift of Faith is a supernatural operation of the Holy Spirit in the experience of the possessor, which enables us to sustain an unwavering trust in God for our personal protection, and for the provisions of our needs.

It is not faith in God, but the **Faith of God** operating in us. God adds to our faith, His Faith---to empower us to believe His Word; this Word that may be so extraordinary, so outrageous---even a suspension of reason, natural laws or science---as with Noah building an ark in the middle of the desert hundreds of miles from water, and telling people that it was going to rain when it hadn't rained before---that's the Gift of Faith.

This gift also manifests to **cast out unclean spirits**. This Gift of the Holy Spirit can only be received after the **Baptism in the Holy Spirit**. Whereas, all mankind has simple faith to believe in Jesus unto Salvation, and to believe the Word and promises of God. But all mankind has this type of faith, otherwise no one would find Jesus and Salvation.

Note: Each Spiritual Gift operates independently of the other. It takes simple faith on our part to operate the gifts. And the Holy Spirit does the rest. For example: We anoint with oil and lay our hands on the sick, and He heals them.

Examples: Through the Gift of Faith, Elijah was told to hide by the brook Cherith, and there the ravens fed him. This was supernatural trust, because ravens are predators and do not feed human beings. Daniel was protected from the lions; Shadrach, Meshach and Abednego were protected from a furnace that was so hot it burnt up the men who fueled it! Angels or the Lord Himself may appear in response to the manifestation of the Gift of Faith.

This gift glorifies God---since without faith it is impossible to please Him. But the Gift of Faith goes far beyond the exercise of simple faith, to overcome powerful demonic opposition. Devils are driven out of people and the blessings of heavenly peace imparted.

Even **The Blessing** is pass down from generation to generation through this gift; the **dead are raised**; and those things that are not materialized as yet appear as though they were already here, when the Holy Spirit declares and decrees a thing through our lips---through this gift we **call those things that be not as though they already are.** The ability to impart the Holy Spirit and Spiritual Gifts is also included in this gift, providing that The Holy Spirit wills it so. In other words, we cannot just "give" or "impart" our gifts or other Spiritual Gifts to people apart from the will of God for that person's life (some ministers say that they can permanently give their Spiritual Gift to whomever they wish, but it is only talk--- spiritual pride on their part).

Working of Miracles

Definition: This gift is the supernatural demonstration of the power of God by which the laws of nature are altered, suspended or controlled (except in the sphere of disease). It was the **sign of the Presence of Jehovah**, and the prophet who wrought a miracle established his divine authority before the people. This gift was a credential. Miracles demonstrates the power of God; healing demonstrates His Agape Love and compassion.

Examples: Before Pharaoh, Moses demonstrated the Working of Miracles; Elijah at Mt. Carmel con-fronted the Baal prophets; Samson killed a lion; Jesus fed 5,000 people; Paul confronted Elymas the sorcerer. The gift can be used as a sign of the Presence and power of God, for the provision of temporal needs, to confirm the preached Word; or give evidence of a divine commission. In the Gifts of Revelation, we participate in the Omniscience of God, the Gifts of Power: Faith, Working of Miracles, and Gifts of Healing, we participate in the Omnipotence (all powerfulness) of God. It's the same power God used to create the world; the same power God exerted when He raised Jesus from the dead. God shares it with us to work miracles through us.

Jesus proclaimed that greater miracles will we do than He did. He means greater in number, because we would have more than 3 ½ years to minister on the earth if we want to serve. Yes, miracles are worked and do not just happen. More times than not an atmosphere of faith, praise worship and agreement followed by the Word of God (Bible message) must take place—where two or three are gathered in His Name, miracles, signs and wonders follow the Word of God.

This is the gift which can bind the raging forces of a storm; can bring a multitude of fish into the nets; can cause a small oil jar to become a fountain of olive oil; and can produce money in a fish's mouth. It's the mighty gift, glorifying the God of all power; stimulating the faith of His people, astonishing and confounding the unbelief of the wicked. We need this power in the Church, the mighty manifestations of God.

Gifts of Healing

Definition: The Gifts of Healing are a manifestation of the Holy Spirit in the sphere of disease. It's not "mind over matter" but supernatural. Gifts of Healing are those healings which God effects by His Holy Spirit. They are NOT to be confused with any human abilities (though God may guide a doctor or surgeon's hand and assist them, it is not this gift operating), but a gift given to the Church for the purpose of removing sicknesses, diseases and infirmities that are the results of Adam's Fall or demonic activity. The term "gifts" is plural. It signifies that the manifestation of the Spirit has several operations: It is a **gift of gifts**, like a cluster of grapes hanging on the vine. As there are classes of diseases: Nerves, muscular, skin, organ, bone, blood, mental etc, so each of the Gifts of Healing has a counteracting effect on some class or ailment.

Examples: Elisha manifested this gift and healed Naaman the Syrian of leprosy; Isaiah healed Hezekiah; Moses through the proxy of the bronze serpent healed the snake-bitten Israelites; Jesus and His disciples healed literally thousands (Jn. 3.14). The Gifts of Healing are often manifested through the **Laying on of Hands** (Mk. 6.5); by the spoken Word (Mt. 8.8); the sacred healing power can be retained and distributed through common fabric (Acts 19.11,12); the Apostle Peter's shadow was used to manifest the Healing Anointing (Acts 5.15).

Sometimes virtue flows unconsciously from the human reservoir, as for instance when the woman touched the hem of Jesus' garment. There are a variety of sicknesses and diseases from which the human race suffers. These possibly can be divided into **twelve groups**, which could also mean there are **twelve Gifts of Healing**. The Book of revelation refers to the **Tree of Life bearing twelve manner of fruit whose leaves are for the healing of the nations** (Rev. 22.1,2).

Prophecy

"But he that prophesies speaks unto men to edification, and exhortation, and comfort. I would that you all speak with Tongues, but rather that you prophesied; for greater is he that prophesies than he that speaks with Tongues, except he interprets, that the church receive edifying" (1 Cor. 14.3, 5).

Prophecy is the first of the three **Gifts of Inspiration**. It is a simple gift, that has often been greatly misunderstood. This is because the term "prophecy" is used both generally and specifically. As stated earlier, the Word of Knowledge and Word of Wisdom is sometimes grouped and believed to be prophecy, when in fact there is very little if any actual prophetic utterance.

In the exercise of the simple gift of Prophecy, some of the other Gifts of revelation may be manifested, but these added gifts must not be confused with the simple gift of prophecy. Prophecy is more than preaching from a prepared text; if this were not so then preachers wouldn't have to prepare sermons! Scripture affirms that God saves people by the avenue of preaching the Gospel, and not by the manifestation of Spiritual Gifts---including Prophecy. But also the gifts of the Spirit are given for signs and wonders which attracts Man's attention towards God. For example, on the Day of Pentecost, when the multitude heard the apostles speaking in other tongues, and understood many of the languages which were spoken; yet not one of these people were converted until Peter stood up and preached the Gospel.

Definition: The general term "Prophecy" means "prediction." "But {on the other hand], the one who prophesies [who interprets the divine will and purpose in **inspired preaching and teaching**] speaks to men for their up-building and constructive spiritual progress and encouragement and consolation…He who prophesies [interpreting the divine will and purpose and teaching with inspiration] edified and improves the church and promotes growth [in Christian wisdom, piety, holiness, and happiness] (1 Cor. 14.3,4 Amp. Bible).

The KJV says **"edification, exhortation, and comfort"** So we see that simple prophecy is not standing up in the midst of the church congregation and declaring that the church is out of Kingdom Order, the pastor is living in sin, or exposing another sister's past, present or future sins! Nor is it a typical sermon about Daniel in the Lion's den and other great Biblical stories.

The Spiritual Gifts of Word of Wisdom or Word of Knowledge may reveal very personal and intimate facts about people, but not with the intent to embarrass, shame, or run them out of the church---but to be delivered privately with love, meekness and humility. This can come within a simple prophetic message.

And though Prophecy may contain Scriptures and sound like a prepared sermon, it is inspired preaching---the Holy Spirit giving the message apart from out studying. If more **Holy Spirit-inspired preaching** was done out of the mouths of preachers, more people would get Saved, and stay Saved; there would be more miracles, and preachers empowered to live what they preach about! The Apostle Paul referring to the edification of the church, wrote: "What shall it profit you, except I speak to you either by **revelation**, or by **knowledge**, or by **prophesying**, or by **doctrine**? (1 Cor. 14.6).

Here Revelation, knowledge, doctrine and Prophecy are given as separate and distinct from each other, so the simple gift of Prophecy obviously doesn't contain the other elements. Prophecy is equal to the Gift of Tongues and Interpretation of Tongues together. One of the greatest books of the Bible to find the operation of several Spiritual Gifts is the Book of Psalms.

To possess the Gift of Prophecy doesn't make us a Prophet or Prophetess. There is a lot more involved in these offices than one Spiritual Gift! Today, so many people are calling themselves Prophets and Prophetesses that the real ones are getting a bad reputation because of the false, inaccurate and lying spirits operating inside these individuals to deceive the Elect into making bad and hurtful decisions. A true Prophet or Prophetess will possess the gift of Prophecy plus many of the Inspiration, Revelation and Power Gifts. The other gifts are needed to fulfill the supernatural office, to speak into the lives of heads of nations---much more miraculous power is needed to change the course of this evil world than "edification, exhortation and comfort."

Examples: A person can be a politician without being a Governor, Senator or President of the United States; a person can be a lawyer without being a judge; so a person can possess the gift of Prophecy without standing in the Office of Prophet or Prophetess. Ministry Gifts (apostle, prophet, evangelist, pastor, teacher) and Spiritual Gifts are not the same thing---neither are the Fruit of the Spirit (the character of God) in the same category.

Tongues

"For he that speaks in an unknown tongue speaks not to men but to God, for no man understands him, because in the Spirit he speaks mysteries 14 For if I pray in an unknown tongue, my spirit prays, but my understanding is unfruitful" (1 Cor. 14.2, 14).

The speaking in unknown or foreign languages is a manifestation of the Holy Spirit, a direct results of being Baptized in or with the Holy Spirit. The Baptism in the Holy Spirit (Acts 2.4) being a second work of Grace upon us, and the Tongues being the evidence of this Baptism. Out of all the Spiritual Gifts, this is the one that has drawn so much controversy in the Body of Christ; dominations draw the line when it comes to Tongues and Interpretation of Tongues, or rather, whether the Baptism in the Holy Spirit is a real work of God or something else. The speaking in other Tongues is a supernatural experience which characterizes the Pentecostal Movement of today. This outpouring is such that **every Christian who is actually filled with the Holy Spirit is heard to speak with other tongues, the Scriptural evidence of the Baptism In The Holy Spirit.**

It is evident that God intended us to recognize the inception of the Holy Spirit by the same manifestation of speaking with other languages. The Spiritual Gift of Tongues is not "learned" knowledge or "mimicked" behavior; one cannot learn to speak in Tongues by reading a book or listening to someone who speaks in Tongues. However, we as a Christian who is Baptized in the Holy Spirit can lay our hands on another Christian, in Agreement, and pray for the other to receive, and Jesus who is truly the Baptizer will make it so. There is no need to beg, travail, fast, or "tarry" for an extended period of time to receive the Baptism in the Holy Spirit with the evidence of speaking in Tongues.

The **Baptism in the Holy Spirit** with the evidence of Tongues is a powerful evidence that we are Saved; this is not to imply that those who do not speak in Tongues are not Saved, but their only evidence is a changed life, which does not always seem apparent in the initial month proceeding Salvation. Sometimes a visible and significant change of behavior and lifestyle doesn't happen for years; but the speaking with Tongues is immediate---we know we are Saved and the Holy Spirit is within.

This is neither to imply that those who speak in Tongues are perfect, sinless, and of good Christian Character immediately after inception, but the **Greater One is within and able to speak out our mouth and make the necessary changes in our world.** Definition: The gift of speaking with unknown Tongues is the power to speak supernaturally by the Holy Spirit, in a language now known to us. We can clearly and correctly articulate in a language the plans, purposes and pursuits of God, speak into being these plans, purposes and pursuits of God.

The **purpose of Tongues** is, firstly, to help us to **worship God.** "He that speaks in an unknown tongue speaks....unto God" (1 Cor. 14.2). Second, the gift **edifies our spirit, soul and body** (v.4) This edification is not just intellectual; but will effect a spiritual building up of ourselves in the Lord. It is also an avenue for **God to speak mysteries**---hidden truths, plans, purposes and pursuits into the earth without Satan comprehending what is spoken, whereby he mounts a resistance to impede God's mission.

"Likewise the Spirit also helps our infirmities for we know not what we should pray for as we ought; but the Spirit Himself makes intercession for us with groaning which cannot be uttered. And He that searches the heart knows what is the mind of the Spirit, because

He makes intercession for the saints according to the will of God" (Rom. 8.27,28).

Another purpose of Tongues is **Personal Prayer**. When we pray in tongues, the Holy Spirit is the initiator of the prayer, and also the One, being God, to answer the prayer. So how can we not get what we are asking for? Think of it this way: God is making a request using a human vessel in order to have the legal right to operate on the earth, seeing that the vessel was born here!

It is the exact way the Trinity (Father/Christ/Holy Spirit) operated in and through the earthborn Son of God, Jesus of Nazareth. It is also true that when we pray in Tongues we may not even be praying for ourselves, but perhaps for someone who is sick and dying 3,000 miles away! **Corporate Prayer** is also an opportunity for God to speak the mysteries into the earth during a church service. We are talking about prayer, and not the Tongues that require an interpreter, to explain to everyone what is said. In individual and corporate prayer, seldom do we know what the congregation is praying about, since there are tremendous needs throughout the world, that we may be distributing supernatural power to.

God can and does use this type of prayer to meet needs even in the remote jungle villages where Missionaries need food, medical supplies, or are in danger from armed militias.

Interpretation of Tongues

"And the whole earth was of one language and one speech. 7 Go to, let Us [Father/Son/Holy Spirit] go down, and there confound their language, that they may not understand one another's speech" (Gen. 11.1,7)

The Spiritual Gift of Interpretation of Tongues is the supernatural ability to translate into a known language what has been spoken in an unknown language. The word "unknown" means unknown to the interpreter and even unknown to others in the meeting. Whereas, there are literally thousands of languages and dialects presently spoken on the earth, and others have become obscure and rarely if ever spoken or heard; still there is the original language that was "confounded" or obscured by God after the building of the **Tower of Babel**; it could very well be the language spoken in Heaven before the world was created and believed to still exist in Heaven.

This language is spoken by God and the holy angels (Satan, fallen angels and demons no long speak or comprehend this language). All these unknown languages can be interpreted by one who has the gift of Interpretation of Tongues. **Interpretation is not necessarily a literal translation**. If the message is from the Holy Spirit, several people with the gift of Interpretation of Tongues may interpret the message using different words according to their individuality, but the jest or conclusion will be the same.

However, only one person at a time should give a message, and one person at a time should give an interpretation; for God is not the author of confusion (1 Cor. 14.26-33). Another thing worth considering: One can give a message in Tongues and activate other Spiritual Gifts within the congregation, whereby another may "see" a vision of what God is saying, another may receive Prophecy, others will have a Word of Wisdom or Word of Knowledge about the subject. So you see, all the Spiritual Gifts can work together because they originate and are distributed severally by the Holy Spirit.

The Anointing

"The Spirit of the Lord God is upon me, because the Lord has anointed me to **preach good tidings** to the meek...to **bind up the brokenhearted**, to proclaim **liberty to the captives**, and **opening of the prison to them that are bound**...to **comfor**t all that mourn... to give unto them **beauty for ashes**, the **oil of joy** for mourning, the **garment of praise** for the spirit of heaviness..." ---Isa. 61.1-30.

But, what exactly is the Anointing. Yes, we know that it destroys the yoke of bondages, but what does the Anointing consist of? It would not be beneficial to have a discussion on Spiritual Gifts without also revealing the Personality and Character of the Triune Godhead Who are the Source of Spiritual Gifts.

Without the Character and Personality of God shining forth we could have mighty Spiritual Gifts but be morally bankrupt, a scoundrel, locked behind prison bars (There are actually incarcerated individuals with God-given Spiritual Gifts that some of our well-known TBN Ministers wish they had!), because their bad character got them into trouble.

"John to the seven churches which are in Asia: Grace be unto you, and peace...and from the **seven Spirits** [sevenfold Holy Spirit] which are before His throne" ---Rev. 1.4.

As we know, the Holy Spirit is a Person, the third member of the triune Godhead. The **seven Spirits (dispositions) of the Holy Spirit is His Personality**, and the Personality of the entire Godhead. **Definition:** The Anointing is God's eternal attributes and abilities to get things done based on His Omniscience (all-knowing), Omnipotence (all-powerful), Omnipresence (everywhere at the same moment of time and eternity), Personality and Character. What we call the Anointing is God's magnificent glorious Self.

Sevenfold Spirits of the Holy Spirit   Isaiah 11.1-5

1. The Spirit of the Lord: Leadership. (Isa. 61.1)
2. "   "   " Wisdom (Pro. 8.5-36; 1 Cor. 1.24).
3. "   "   " Understanding (1 Ki. 3.12; Dan. 2.21).
4. "   "   " Counsel (Ps. 33.11,12; Isa. 9.7)
5. "   "   " Might (1 Chr. 29.12; Eph. 3.14-20).
6. "   "   " Knowledge (Pro. 1.7; Hos. 4.6).
7. "   "   " Fear (Reverence) Pro. 9.10).

These attributes comprise the basic Personality of God. This is why God can be known by human beings, inasmuch as our minds can grasps these definite attributes and communicate on a mental level. It is also the reason why the Gospel made sense to our minds even when we were spiritually dead, we had common ground with God---Personality.

The Fruit of the Spirit: Character of God

As stated earlier, having good Christian Character will draw more people to Christ then all the Spiritual Gifts combined. We cannot use our Spiritual Gifts to persuade a judge and jury, break out of jail or prison---because the Holy Spirit actually controls them---not us! If our character becomes so bad that it comes to the attention of the courts, the Holy Spirit may allow the judge to give us a long vacation!

The first responsibility of the Holy Spirit once indwelled in us is not to minister to those outside us but to our own soul which houses the **Intellect, Emotions, Will and Imagination facilities**. The Process of Sanctification---the renewing of our mind is the first priority of the Holy Spirit. Purifying the vessel is so important, otherwise the Anointing can be corrupted by the mental and emotional baggage we possess.

Many false prophecies have come forth whereby ruining Christian marriages, courtships, ministries, careers, businesses and social relationships. This happens because our vessel is immature, dirty, stressed-out, have our own strong opinions, unconsecrated, or have our own agenda about the people involved. Here is where the scrubbing and cleaning of the stained clay vessel, the character rebuilding begins.

"But the fruit of the [Holy] Spirit [the work which His Presence within accomplishes] is love, joy (gladness), peace, patience (an even temper, forbearance), kindness, goodness (benevolence), faithfullness,

23 Gentleness (meekness, humility), self-control (self-restraint, continence). Against such things there is no law [that can bring a charge]."

1. Love Jn. 3.16 1 Cor. 13 Gal. 5.6
2. Joy (Gladness) Ps. 16.11; 30.5 1 Pet. 1.8
3. Peace Ps.119.165 Isa. 9.6
4. Longsuffering (Patience) Ex. 34.6 Col. 1.11
5. Gentleness (Kindness)2 Cor. 10.1 Eph. 2.7
6. Goodness Ps. 23.6 Ro. 11.22 Eph. 5.9
7. Faith (Faithfulness) Lam. 3.23 1 Cor. 1.9
8. Meekness Zep. 2.3 1 Tim. 6.11 Jam. 1.21
9. Temperance (Self-Control) Acts 24.25 2 Pet. 1.6

The Price of the Anointing

This is not where the Author (Me) tells you to go get in the $500 offering line at church. The Anointing cannot be bought and sold to the biggest tither (as many pastors want us to believe).

"Wait and listen, everyone who is thirsty! Come to the waters, and he who has no money, come buy [priceless, spiritual] wine and milk **without money** and without price [**simply for the self-surrender that accepts the blessing**]" ---Isa. 55.1-3.

Salvation is free; but it cost Jesus His mortal life and it cost us in other ways: One of the ways it cost is the death of the self-life, the old man and his sinful lifestyle, thinking and ways. Another is: We are persecuted by Satan, religious people and the unsaved world. Spiritual Gifts, the Anointing is like-wise free, but comes with even more persecution. It is not tagged with a material cost but a spiritual cost. The point is, are we willing to count the spiritual cost and pay the spiritual price?

If so, we are usable to God and Spiritual Gifts will come. Now, it's about providing a clean vessel for all these Spiritual Gifts. Gifts aren't earned---that's why they're called gifts. But there is a few things we can do to make the activation of Spiritual Gifts easy for our Partner, the Holy Spirit to accomplish in us.

1. Pro. 15. 33 Be humble.
2. Pro 11.2 When pride comes, so does shame.
3. Ps. 63. 1,2 Be thirsty and earnestly seek Him.
4. Ps. 92.1 Give thanks to Him.
5. Isa. 55.1 Come drink at the waters.
6. Isa. 58.6 The fast that looses the heavy burdens.
7. Zec. 10.1 Ask for the Holy Spirit.
8. Ps. 35.13 Humble your soul with fasting.
9. Lk. 2.37 Prayer and fasting as a way of life.
10. Jn. 8.32,36 Know the Truth and be set free.
11. 1 Jn. 1.9 Repent, confess sins.
12. Ro. 6.1-14 Learn to yield to the Holy Spirit.
13. 2 Cor. 13.14 Fellowship with the Holy Spirit.

14. Mk. 10.30 Blessings come with persecution.
15. Ro. 8.35 Nothing shall separate us.

CHAPTER FOUR

Spiritual Warfare/Spiritual Freedom

"The pride of your heart has deceived you..."---Obad. 1.3.

Let us not leave any stone unturned to get to the source of so much wretchedness. Why is it that most of us Christians have no power over sin in our lives? We are not only talking about the leadership falling into disgrace, but the rest of us---maybe not on the evening news---but nevertheless falling short of the glory and expectations of God. We need more power for our Christian Life. One of the weapons in Satan's arsenal of evil is spiritual pride.

Pride is not only one of his weapons, it was the main reason he was thrown out of Heaven. Therefore, pride is a part of his personality; it is very powerful when working in the self-life of human beings. It makes no difference whether the human being is a Christian or not, spiritual pride operates through the Law of Sin and Death, and is a personality defect that has to be dealt with in our Christian Life. What exactly is deception? Obviously it is the process or state of being deceived.

The Webster Dictionary describes it as, "To believe what is false or invalid; to be misled; or to be ensnared; to deliberately misrepresent facts by works or actions in order to further one's own interest; other, beguile, mislead, delude."

The biblical example of this phenomenon is recorded in Gen. 3.13, where Eve confessed, "The serpent beguiled {(deceived, tricked} me, and I did eat." She was the first human being to be deceived; though in Heaven, the serpent, being Satan, introduced deception to the angelic realm, and was cast out of Heaven because of it: "Satan which deceives the whole world (Rev. 12.9).

Cain was too proud to take even God's advice and rethink his present course of action, and line up with the acceptable Word of God. God told him that a deceiver, the spirit of pride was crouched like a tiger outside his door; it was waiting to devour him; but God counseled Cain not to give in to the evil spirit, but resist it by Faith and confidence in the revealed Word of God.

However, Cain did not take God seriously, but went out and killed Abel. He ruined his Calling and Commission, his opportunity at ministering to humanity. There are many ways that a spirit of pride can enter us, but it is first introduced through some type of deception, a single or set of lies, values, postulates, theories, philosophies or beliefs, that we have reckoned as unquestionable truth, and are making important decisions based on them; which means that we gave the spirit of deception control of us and our ministry decisions through this "hook" that this spirit has in our heart.

For example, we may not believe that women can be effective ministers based on what we think of women who have hurt us, or a mother that was, controlling, emotional or mentally unstable. It's not that we hate women, but we don't believe that they are emotionally equipped to handle the demands of pasturing a church and counseling hurting people; and so we come up with this "reasonable" explanation that seems "biblical" when in fact it is demonic!

The spirit of deception can also opens the door to rebellion, which lets in a spirit of pride, and pride will cause us to be insanely affixed on ourselves, our physical appearance, finances, family successes, linage, vocations, degrees, social and political connections, material property, vehicles, our "stadium-size "ministry, and our "perceived" popularity.

We become more interested in acquiring loyal "fans" than saving souls and mentoring young ministers. Sometimes we are patted on the back by our fans so much that we walk slightly bent over! Yet we are spiritual criminals. We strut around with our armed body guards when the real enemy is within us; we are the one most hazardous to our health; we are the one toxic to those around us; and we are the one who need to be delivered. We preach and people throw money at our feet; we are on television as a Christian celebrity. We believe our own hype and publicity. We have forgotten where we came from, as sinners, and Who it was who loved and saved us. We are more concerned with selling books, CDs and other merchandise than the sick, seniors, addicts and others in need.

Many of us are terrified to use our fortune and connections to help a struggling minister or ministry, for fear that minister will one day become as prosperous as us, an equal, or yet, a better minister that us; so we don't help them in order to keep them looking up to us; we make them promises with no intentions of keeping them: "They must remain a fan."

In Num. 32.23 warns us that "…your sins shall find you out. Whatever spirit drives us will one day expose us for the person that we really are, that is, the person we have become. It's the duty and nature of evil spirits to deceive and then expose us; as a toaster toast bread because it was manufactured for that purpose, so is the evil spirit of pride bent on exposing us.

The Word in Pro. 16.18 confirms this: "Pride goes before destruction, and a haughty spirit before a fall. And 1 Cor. 10.12 reads:"Wherefore let him who thinks he stands take heed lest he fall."

Spiritual pride paralyzes the leadership, and then the congregation are little more than worshippers of the leader and not true worshippers of Christ---making flesh our arm to lean on. If we think that we are all that and a bag of potato chips we are mistaken. If we persist in this type of behavior, the Word says "take heed" because we are about to fall---and hard! Few ministers fully recover their status and ministry after a national scandal. God may still use us, but not nearly as much as before.

For example, we may go from preaching to 300 million souls worldwide, down to preaching to fifty souls in a small church. The spirit of pride releases a strange power and counterfeit anointing in the congregation, and we find ourselves deceived into believing that it is the Presence of the Holy Spirit. Even counterfeit prophetic utterances come forth in such a pseudo environment; we become more enslaved, bound to that ministry---not because God told us to stay there---but because of witchcraft!

Spiritual pride opens the door for other spirits to enter the leader and the congregation; these spirits include religious spirits, lying, greed, jealousy perversion, sickness, disease and other hateful demons. As deceived leaders we proclaim that "Everything you need is in the house!" We said it to imply that we have all the Spiritual Gifts, spiritual knowledge, wisdom, mantles, divine revelation and counsel. This is a lie.

We said it to keep our people from experiencing the fullness of Jesus' manifestations in other ministries; we said it because of insecurity; we want our membership not to give money, time and presence elsewhere; also, as leaders we already know that other ministers in the area have Spiritual Gifts, mantles, teaching and preaching skills that we are envious of, and so we discourages our members from experiencing the power of Christ that blankets the entire Body.

Pride in a Christian

The following are examples of Spiritual Pride: Deceived to think we are self-sufficient; Feel that we don't need the Church; Want to be a leader but doesn't need the training; Will not receive instruction, correction and is un-teachable; The leaders are always wrong and we are always right; We are perfect as we are.

We rebel against civil and Christian authority; Have an inflated opinion of self; thinks everyone else is less spiritual, less intelligent, inferior or ignorant; Can't face the biblical truth about ourselves; Think we know the Bible better than everyone; Blames others for our failures; Won't take personal responsibility; Is selfish and self-glorious, or think we are "fabulous."

We Claim to "daily" receive "personal" visitations from Jesus, extraordinary visions or being taught personally by Jesus (as Paul was); Seldom repents even when caught doing wrong; justifies or minimizes; Claims to discover better or additional ways to hear from God, like the Koran, Masons, Horoscope, meditation and eastern philosophies; Lacks self-discipline, control, an indulger in vices, but claim we are strong and these vices don't affect us like other Christians; Claim that we are the only one in our church that is Saved; Claim that all we need is Jesus and the King James Version Bible; Claim that we don't need to fast, pray, counseling, Inner Healing & Deliverance, because we are at some high level of Faith; Claim that we never sin; Claim to been granted an extraordinary title like: Exalted Bishop Chief-Apostle, and similar titles (Jesus Christ is the only Chief Apostle).

Combating Pride

"God resist the proud, but gives grace unto the humble.

7 Submit your selves therefore to God. Resist the devil, and he will flee from you.

8 Draw near to God, and He will draw near to you"---Jam. 34.6,7,8.

Humility is the key to getting set free from the spirit of pride. If Cain would have humbled himself and listened to God, he would not have stepped out the door and been overwhelmed by the crouched tiger of pride. Humility of self allows the Grace---unmerited favor---and power of God to cleanse the consciousness by the washing and regeneration of the Word.

The Word will cleanse the mind from the demonically imposed sin-consciousness which is under the Law of Sin and Death, that is, a consciousness riddled with condemnation, guilt, shame, regret and other negative emotions---to a righteousness consciousness which is under the Law of the Spirit of Life. Humility involves our submission to God, our activation of Faith in God and His Word to resist the Devil and his spirit of pride; he will have no legal right or hook in us, and will have to, by the Law of the Spirit of Life, leave us alone. As we draw near to God he draws near to us too; this decreases the ministry time tremendously, by bridging the gap-time between our distorted mind, and His Christ-Mind, Inner Healing and Deliverance power.

Fasting, prayer and reading the Word is the best way to draw near to God. We must sanctify ourselves, separate ourselves from the corrupting connections to the world---those connections that feed the prideful spirit; even a separation from the influences of other vain and conceited people whom we hang out with or associate with after work, in a lodge, frat or sorority house. Repentance of pride and a sincere desire to change our lifestyle under the guidance of the Holy Spirit will start the cleansing process. a part of the local church is scriptural.

Being under authority, possibly re-turning and apologizing to the church leader that God placed us under is also a good start. For the Word says to, "obey them that have the rule over you..." (Heb. 13.17). Fellowship and faithful service to the ministry will break the back of the spirit of pride and remove self-centered selfishness; as to "not forsaking the assembly of ourselves together... "---Heb.10.25.

The seeking and obtaining of Inner Healing and Deliverance can be described as this: "Let us draw near with a true heart in full assurance of faith, having our hearts sprinkled from an evil conscious, and our bodies washed with pure water" (Heb. 10.22. Inner Healing and Deliverance is the children's bread!

"Thy Word have I hid in mine heart, that I might not sin against Thee"---Ps. 119.11.

It does not go without mentioning, that we as Christians have a certain amount of "mental ascent" when it comes to the Word of God. We read and understand what the Bible teaches, but do not put that understanding into practice; whereas, the Word of God must be more than a philosophical idea but action; from action to practice, and from practice to a lifestyle.

The deception and pride can be eliminated through Repentance, Faith and Prayer. But all these must be rooted in the Word of God, to have any lasting effect, because the Holy Spirit only operates by and through the Word of God. If we wanted to be set free from whatever it is that binds us, what keeps us from living successfully in the Word, the Word of God must be taken seriously. Then we will be successful, prosperous and capable of fulfilling our destiny, the Calling and Commissioning that is on our life. To begin with, we must be specific and stand on God's Word as the foundation of our thoughts, emotions, will, and imaginations (creativity); and pray according to the Word of God. The best way to pray according to the Word of God is to study the New Covenant, the Word of God as written in the New Testament.

To conquer indwelling demon spirits that have latched onto us like swamp leeches, we must specifically follow the Word of God. In Mt. 4.4, Jesus states, "It is written, Man shall not live by bread alone, but by every word that proceeds out of the mouth of God." Jesus made this statement in response to an attack on His mind, will, emotion and empty, fasted stomach.

Satan tempted Jesus to use His authority solely to validate Himself, to satisfy his stomach, and to learn more about the "mystery" of the "Seed" that had been hidden from him for ages (Col. 1.26) prompted the curiosity of Satan. Initially, he wasn't 100% certain that Jesus is the Son. Whereas, Jesus told Him that He was the Son of God because He refused to do what Satan told him! He was the only Man who could resist Satan.

Jesus told him that all He was required to do was the will of His Father who sent Him. He wouldn't perform miracles solely for the sake of proving who He is, never before the one He came to destroy the works of. "Then the devil takes Him up into the holy city, and sets Him on the pinnacle of the temple, and says to Him, If you are the Son of God, cast yourself down; for it is written, He shall give His angels charge concerning thee…" (Mt. 4.6,7).

This took place after Jesus refused to turn the stones into food. Now, Satan tempted Jesus to put God to a foolish test concerning the Father's love, ability or willingness to protect His Son from danger or death.

"Again, the devil takes Him up into an exceeding high mountain, and shows Him all the kingdoms of the world, and the glory of them. And says unto Him, All these things will I give thee, if thou will fall down and worship me" (V. 8-11).

Jesus' response was most fittingly an example for us. He told the devil to get lost! More King James-like, "get thee hence." The devil took Jesus up on the mountain to show Him the "glory" the pride of owning the whole world, everything and everyone in it. It was pride that Satan wielded before Jesus, the same pride that got him thrown out of Heaven. He boasted of how it was handed to him (by Adam) and that he was in control of it; and all Jesus had to do to get it---NOW---was to bow down and worship him; Jesus didn't dispute his claim. Many times, as Christians, Satan takes us up and sits us on a high pedestal and promises to give us what our flesh craves---popularity, money, power or sex---if we would bow down and worship him.

He is able, via his territorial spirits, to deliver what he promises; but God is also able to deliver the promised judgment upon those of us who live for the devil and die in him---that judgment is Hell. But the answer to this dilemma lies in Jesus' response: "Thou shall worship the Lord thy God, and Him only shall thou serve" (v.10). The goal of Satan is to get us to worship him; when we fall into sin and stay there, we are worshipping him.

The occasional fall is not worship, but the habitual revisiting becomes a habit, then a lifestyle. The next thing we know we are far away from the narrow road. And so, as Jesus utilized the Word of God to combat the advances of Satan, we can also use the Word of God to protect, deliver and rescue us from his temptations and traps. When we speak and pray the Word of God, tremendous power is released in our lives, power to destroy yokes and lift burdens.

Because the Word of God is a two-edged sword and our tongue is the member that wields it, we have to be careful that we are not just speaking the Word but doers of it too. If not, the same sword that loops of the heads of demons (figuratively) will loop our head off too! Inasmuch, as we are subject to obey the Word as demons are. Jesus was (and still is) a Man of Prayer; His life was one of fasting, prayer and fellowship with the Father.

He knows the worth of prayer---that it is priceless—and passes this truth on to us. Many times He had to get away from the crowds to spend time with the Father; the people, hungry for the Word, pressed in so that He had little time to eat, pray or even sleep. Every great manifestation of God's Glory in the Old and New Testament was in response to fervent prayer. Abraham, Moses, David, Solomon, the Prophets and Apostles prayed the glory of God down, and changed their circumstances. After David committed adultery and murdered Uriah, Bathsheba's husband, he prayed this prayer of godly sorrow and repentance:

1 "Have mercy upon me, O God, according to thy loving kindness; according unto the multitude of thy tender mercies blot out my transgressions.

2 Wash me thoroughly from mine iniquity, and cleanse me from my sin.

3 For I acknowledge my transgressions; and my sin is ever before me.

7 Purge me with hyssop, and I shall be clean; wash me, and I shall be whiter than snow"---Ps. 51.1-3,7.

David is a good example of a man who did some lowdown, scandalous things, but when his head cleared, he realized what he had done and repented. Yet, according to God, David was a man after His own heart! David was human; so are we. And all that God requires when we sin is Repentance and Faith; both of these can be accomplished through humble prayer.

One reason why it is so hard for many of us to pray like David is because we are more sorry that we got caught then we are of the sin. We are reeling from the blow and effects of private or public disgrace than from godly sorrow. Still many of us find it hard to pray because of the spirit of pride saying, "You are pathetic!" And so the spirit of pride won't allow us to pour out our heart to the Lord and ask for forgiveness and cleansing which is also Inner Healing and Deliverance.

This is where the good fight of Faith comes in! If we really want to be delivered, we don't care with the demons say or what the people around us think. People don't know what we are going through; they don't know how good God has been to us; they weren't there when He saved our soul; and they weren't there when the rent, light bill, gas bill, phone bill and the car note was due; not to mention they weren't there when the cupboard was bare and our wallet was empty: But God showed up and He delivered us from the trials, tribulations, situations, snares, addictions and from criminals!

Saints, God knows what we need to get back on track. In Jn. 16.23, He says to "Ask, Seek and Knock." Having Faith in God we ask for cleansing, Inner Healing and Deliverance; we seek first the Kingdom and its righteousness believing that all the other things we need will be added accordingly.

We speak words impregnated with Faith, what the Word of God says concerning our addictions or weaknesses, and know for certain that we will receive according to our Faith; that God has already blessed us with ALL spiritual blessings in heavenly places and on earth in Christ Jesus (Eph. 1.3). Everything that we will ever need in this journey is provided by our Lord. Prayer is the act of "walking by faith and not by sight," as Paul wrote in 2 Cor. 5.7).

Knowing that God's Word is true and unchanging, we apply it to our particular problem; we also know that the Word of God is Fact and not a feeling; nor is it the power of the intellect or an act of our will--- though we engage our intellect and will in a quality decision to act on the Word of God. Faith comes by hearing, acknowledging and putting into practice the Word.

It is not putting God to a foolish test when putting Him in remembrance of His promises. It's not that God forgets anything, but quoting His Word back to Him---or out loud in the earth---places a definite time for the fulfillment of that promise, for God who lives in eternity outside of time. We become the point of contact, being both an eternal and finite being where time and eternity meet within our Physical Body. Then God can and will answer the prayer, because He has our permission, our petition or request, the legal right to interfere in our life.

Faith declared, "I have it NOW! Hope declares, "I will have it!" Mental assent declares, "The Word states that I should have it but I don't see it!" Also, mental assent, which is basically human reasoning declares, "I must have sinned (again) and that's why I don't have my petition!" Lasting Recovery involves genuine Faith; without Faith it is impossible to please God (Heb. 11.6). Do we fully grasp what the word "impossible" means? Neither does Hope please God, though it is the object of our Faith (what we want from God). And mental assent doesn't please God or move His hand to help us. All mental assent can do is think of reasons why the Word doesn't work for us, or why God is withholding His promises. Mental assent is the mental processes without the input of the human spirit; it is actually the self-life maneuvering to get back on the throne of our life. As it stands, as Born Again Believers, Christ sits on the throne of our life and self is at His feet; the self wants to again be the ruler, with Christ setting at his feet, or out the door!

In the same way that Abraham was fully persuaded that God's promises and His oaths were realities, we must believe: Adhere to, trust in and rely on His promises and His ability and willingness to perform them admirably.This implies not considering the outer situations, circumstances or appearances. But give praise, worship and thanks to God BEFORE the results come, BEFORE the healing, BEFORE the deliverance, and BEFORE the finances arrive.

"Do not fret or have any anxiety about anything, but in every cir-cumstance and in everything, by prayer and petition (definite requests), with thanksgiving, continue to make your wants known to God.

7 And God's peace {shall be yours, that tranquil state of a soul assured of its salvation through Christ, and so fearing nothing from

God...} which transcends all understanding shall garrison and mount guard over your hearts and minds in Christ Jesus" Phil. 4.6,7.

Faith is believing God's Word; Fear is believing Satan's word. Herein the key to receiving answered prayer: Faith and definite requests to God, believing that we have already received before we actually make the requests. Because we believe that God loves us and already answered our prayer, we rest assured in that tranquil state of praise and worship---fearing nothing that the demons may bring to slow down or stop our blessing---until we see the manifestation of our prayer.

Having peace that transcends all understanding, drives the demons out! Fearing nothing that comes our way in life is the results of Faith in God; living according to the Word of God goes hand-in-hand with Faith. We cannot have genuine Faith in God and not adhere to, trust in and rely on His revealed Word. Knowing that God cares for us lovingly, affectionately, and watchfully makes it easier to go to Him for Forgiveness, Inner Healing and Deliverance.

Most of us wouldn't confess to anyone we believe would kill us when we are done. And that is what the Devil wants us to think about God. So he tells us to hide our sins, suppress or hide our addictions, indulgences, urges and thinking distortions instead of getting help.

Then one day he springs the trap and the whole world knows what we have been doing more or less all of our life! Jos. 1.8 advises us not to let the Word of God depart from our mouth; and the only way it will be in the mouth is that it first be abundantly in the heart; for out of the abundance of the heart {human spirit's intuition, intellect, emotions, will, imagination} the mouth will speak. Then we'll experience soul prosperity.

Praying according to the Word, which is hidden in our heart, keeps us from habitually sinning. Another great principle to consider is written in Mat. 18.18 (Amp. Bible). "Truly I tell you, whatever you forbid and declare to be improper and unlawful on earth must be what is already forbidden in heaven, and whatever you permit and declare proper and lawful on earth must be what is already permitted in heaven." The Standard for what is unlawful or improper is in relation to the Word of God. Evil, the entire works of Satan has been declared unlawful everywhere except in Hell.

When we pray the perfect will of God "Thy will be done in earth as it is in heaven," we are requesting that the same Standard be invoked here on earth that is the Spiritual Law and legal state environment in Heaven. For example: There is no sicknesses, diseases, addictions or criminal activity in heaven, and so we can declare and decree ourselves legally free (as the fruit of Salvation) of all of these bondages on earth.

And the second part of the verse affirms the legal status of Heaven with our free will to declare and decree freedom according to the Spiritual Law of the Spirit of Life, the legal state of Heaven that is free from evil and its consequences. For whom the Son of God has set free is free indeed! Addictions know no boundaries: Age, race, gender, social status, the Saved and un-Saved fall victim to drugs, alcohol, tobacco, sexual addictions, and deviant, antisocial behaviors. However, we as Christians have a resource available that others do not have: A Covenant relationship with God. It is a matter of if we want to remain a Victim or achieve Victory. Because God can turn a mess into a message, a test into a testimony, a trial into a triumph, and a victim into a victory.

Sometimes we think that God is going to do everything for us, that He can somehow "force us" to follow the Word. But that is not the truth. God did not force us to get Saved nor will He force us to stay Saved. God, through Jesus Christ and the Holy Spirit are Covenant Partners with us. As Partners, the Trinity will not and cannot do all of the work; we have to purposely engage our will and cooperate with our Partners. And as the Three are One in Spirit, we don't have to satisfy three different Persons, but One. Nevertheless, we pray to the Father in Jesus' Name because He told us too.

Mat. 18.19 (Amp. Bible) concludes and establishes that the action must began with us, on earth, and not in Heaven at the throne of God: "Again I tell you, if two of you on earth agree (harmonize together, make a symphony together) about whatever {anything and everything} they may ask, it will come to pass and be done for them by My Father in heaven."

Two Christians in agreement can turn the table on the Devil and erase a multitude of sins. Herein lies the authority and power of the Believer to destroy yokes and lift heavy burdens. Hiding our sins isn't the answer; it is like a closet full of filthy clothes that as time passes stinks up the whole house; or worst, a refrigerator, that has been turned off for months but full of raw meat, then opened! Getting sins forgiven, washed away and their outworking consequences made none and void is the ideal goal.

Therefore, we come into agreement with one another, bind the demonic spirits responsible for the sicknesses or addictions on earth, and God in Heaven honors our decisions and causes them to be tangible in our life.

God knows what we have need of before we ask; nevertheless, we ask that He may enter into our life. Ask and you shall receive, is what Jesus taught; also, have Faith in God, or have the Faith of God by speaking positive words of Faith, and call those things that be not as yet as though they already exist in the natural realm. Walking by Faith and not by sight is what we are talking about. If we believe that God's Word is true we have to live by it. This will cause our Faith to grow from the mustard seed kind to the great Faith that Jesus spoke of concerning the Roman centurion.

Though everyone has been dealt a measure of Faith in order to get Saved in the first place, not everyone uses their Faith to get Saved, but use it to follow other religions and philosophies; but Faith increases by hearing, acknowledging and putting into practice the Word of God. Fear creates doubt: Doubt comes by hearing and practicing unbelief, false religions and philosophies. So we have to practice being positive in our thinking and don't give up on ourselves or recovery. This is done by praying the solution and not complaining to God, ourselves or to friends about the problem.

Every thought or action must mirror and confirm what we believe God for. Being vigilant, lest a negative mental image of failure stay in the conscious mind too long and become a permanent fixture! If doubt, which is a vain imagination comes into the mind, rebuke it, and it will burst like a bubble. Summit to God, resist the Devil and he will flee (Jam. 4.7).

"Because when they knew and recognized Him as God, they did not honor and glorify Him as God or give Him thanks. But instead they became futile and godless in their thinking {with vain imagining, foolish reasoning and stupid speculations} and their senseless minds were darkened. 22 Claiming to be wise, they became fools..." ---Ro. 1.21,22.

The imagination is the facility of the soul that is capable of con-ceiving and grasping abstract ideas, concepts, theories and principles. It enables us to plan today for a possible tomorrow (which is not promised to any of us). The imagination is also the facility of the soul that can create art, literature, music, build and construct things that have never existed before; it is also the facility that we use to dream at night, daydream or fantasize. But imagination corrupted by the flesh, world or demons, becomes the facility used to create paranoia—fearful, terrifying and paralyzing thoughts that people are after us to do harm when they are not; it also creates doubt, unbelief, religious error, racism, sexual fantasy, lust, pride, vanity, self-importance and self-righteousness; these are examples of vain imaginations. Vain imaginations are often projected into our minds by the territorial spirits; often it is done during the sleep state, meditations or daydreaming period when the mind is idle and open. Certain Eastern meditation techniques relax the mind as to become vulnerable to psychic attacks from demons.

God has imagination too; His is called divine imaginations. Through His facility He sends us what we call visions and dreams. This is one of God's primary methods of communication. Divine imaginations is God sending us mental images (pictures) of our future or visual information about others; He also sends us visual information about local or world situations and circumstances, our destiny and Calling, His plans, purposes and pursuits using us or just the overall plan; He also sends visions of Himself so that we can personally know Him.

The mind of God is like a television station. He sends out powerful visual images with an audible tract containing information about who He is, and His plans. These images may be real time or future; and since God always is in the present, He knows what is destined to happen throughout human history. Those who are sensitive and close to God see visions from God; God is no respecter of persons; He will talk to anyone who will listen!

"Be well balanced (temperate, sober of mind), be vigilant and cautious at all times; for that enemy of yours, the devil, roams around like a lion roaring {in fierce hunger}, seeking someone to seize upon and devour. 9 Withstand him; be firm in faith…"1 Pet. 5.8,9.

The biggest deception that Satan has pulled off since the Garden of Eden is to convince humanity that he doesn't exist. The Word of God declares that there is such a person as Satan or the Devil, and that he is alive and living on Earth. He is not as powerful as he was before Calvary, since the decisive victory won by Jesus Christ, but he still remains the most notorious murderer, liar and trickster that has even lived. But those who are In Christ Jesus, have weapons to fight against this entity. Knowing this, we are not ignorant of his devices and tactics. Satan moves and maneuvers in the Psychic or Mental Realm, the realm of the senses; he also uses subtle suggestions, deceptions and delusions. One thing for sure, his implanted thoughts do not line up with the Word of God and can be easily discerned by those of us who diligently study the Bible. But, during the years when we didn't know the Word of God, was when Satan got his foothold.

Now we have to be more conscious of our thought processes, motives, desires and reasoning to make sure we are not being lured into one of his traps. We have to cast down and reject dreams, visions, false prophecies or personal feelings that don't line up with the Word. We also have to practice resisting the "doubting Thomas'" of the local churches and the world.

As doubting Thomas' we sound so knowledgeable when we say: "Once an alcoholic, always an alcoholic, or "Once a drug addict, always a drug addict"---which is NOT the Word of God concerning New Creatures in Christ Jesus; this thinking distortion is also extend ed to other moral failures as a reason not to help fallen Christians get back on their feet; it is also proclaiming that the Blood of Jesus Christ is powerless to deliver addicts or certain people, therefore doubting the effectiveness of the Word of God.

And so we would rather use this excuse to shoot the fallen Christians like injured horses! Jesus Christ took upon Himself our grief, sicknesses, weaknesses and distresses, even the pains and consequences of punishment, and with the stripes that wounded Him we are healed and made whole (Isa. 53.4).

In so doing, He not only secured eternal Salvation for those who believe in him, but Healing and Deliverance from the molestation of unclean spirits. That is why the weapons of our warfare are not physical weapons, but mighty and effective to demolish strongholds of every kind; there is no bondage that the Holy Spirit cannot break; and the only person that He cannot save is the one who doesn't want to get Saved. For the most part, thoughts are formed in the brain by observation, association, and teaching.

Though it is difficult to avoid hearing other people's opinions, we can nevertheless avoid soul ties with them, certain places, programs and reading printed materials that is contrary to Christian belief, that doesn't support our confess-ion of Faith, Healing and Deliverance.

Face it, if we want to stop drinking we have to stop buying liquor, going to bars and clubs and hanging out with people who drink! Why? Because we are saying one thing and doing another; we are not making arrangements to stop but to continue drinking. This principle applies to all addictions, strongholds, habits or thinking distortions: Feed your Faith and starve your Doubts to death!

Whatever you feed will get the fattest; whatever you starve will eventually die. Thinking positively is not a new idea. Non-Christian motivational speakers have capitalized on this concept, and perhaps have helped a lot of depressed people; they have also created a lot of multimillion and billionaires too. But positive thinking alone will not change the core of us, though it will alter many thinking patterns. Here is where the Word of God and prayer comes in, the help of the powerful, life-changing Holy Spirit.

Not letting the Word depart from before our eyes and heart is the key to confessing the truth in the earth about who we are, and the positive confession of our destiny with our mouth. And God will make His Word good if we diligently act upon it. We make every prayer a confession of Faith, and don't undo those prayers by listening to the "speculations," the vain imaginations of our mind whose goal is to return to the familiar, that former state of pleasure and freedom from God, that state of thinking that it's okay to sin as long as it's temporary; or, "I'm Saved, so I can sin and not lose my Salvation... or I am the Bishop, and so..."

We pray to the Father in the Name of Jesus (Jn. 16.23); there isn't another way to approach God and be accepted by Him. Because of our confidence in Jesus, the Father answers and grants our petitions.

Our praying authority comes from Jesus, the High Priest of the Heavenly Sanctuary (Acts 3.12). Without the use of His Name, we are stuck, like other religions, with a form of godliness without the actual relationship and power to overcome adversity---mainly, our adversary the Devil, and our wicked desires to please our flesh. Prayer is planting the seed of Faith to claim our harvest!

Types of Prayers

There are many types of prayers and ways to pray; since this is not a book on prayer only, we will discuss a few.

The Prayer of Faith is described in many ways and places in the New Testament. Prayer for the Christian is based on the New Testament Covenant. We should not pray like David prayed under the Old Testament Covenant of Law--- that God would kill our enemies. But under Grace there is forgiveness and mercy.

In Mk. 11.24 it states, "Therefore I tell you, whatever you ask for in prayer, believe that you have received it, and it will be yours." Jesus proclaimed, "Have Faith in God." Another translation says, "Have the Faith of God," which also makes sense because God does everything through the exercise of His Faith. He has dealt to everyone a measure, a degree, a mustard seed of His divine Faith. God, through Faith, calls those things that be not as though they already were; this is the Prayer based and rooted in Faith---to call those things that be not as yet as though they already exist.

In Eph. 6.10-17, the Apostle Paul gave a discourse on spiritual warfare. From there he immediately wrote of prayer being an essential part of that spiritual warfare: "Pray at all times (on every occasion, in every season) in the Spirit, with all {manner of} prayer and entreaty" Eph 6.18 (Amp).

The Prayer of Consecration is another type of prayer that is widely described and used in the New Testament Covenant. To consecrate means to sanctify, separate for a divine purpose. We as Christians are a people set aside by God. We are members of His divine family, the Church, the Bride of Christ, the fruit, being the children of the Resurrection. Therefore, we are separated from the world, and do separate ourselves by uttering this type of prayer.

We declare and decree aloud that we belong to Christ and He belongs to us! In the upper room, Jesus consecrated the wine and the bread through prayer. "And as they were eating, Jesus took bread, and blessed it, and brake it, and gave it to the disciples, and said, "Take, eat, this is my body. And He took the cup, and gave thanks, and gave it to them, saying, Drink ye all of it. For this is my blood of the New Testament" (Mat. 28.26-28). In Jn. 17.15-17 (Amp. Bible), Jesus consecrated, set apart disciples for a special purpose: "I do not ask that You take them out of the world, but that You will keep and protect them from the evil one. They are not of the world (worldly, belonging to the world), {just} as I am not of the world. Sanctify them {purify, consecrate, separate them for Yourself, make them holy} by the Truth; Your word is Truth."

In further verses, Jesus consecrated Himself and future Believers in the Body of Christ, so that we are also sanctified, purified, separated and wholly consecrated to and In Him. In the same way the Father sent Jesus into the world, Jesus sends us into the world with the same consecration through prayer.

Prayer of Commitment: "Delight your-self also in the Lord, and He will give you the desires and secret petitions of your heart. Commit your ways to the Lord {roll and repose each care of your load on Him}; trust (lean on, rely on, and be confident) also in Him and He will bring it to pass" (Ps. 37.4,5 Amp. Bible). It is obvious that the Prayer of Commitment involves our spiritual relationship with God.

It is our commitment to Him, not His commitment to us that is involved. God is faithful; and we are not always faithful, though we try with all our might. Many times are burdens are so heavy that we cannot lift them; that is when we roll or drag them to the cross. Then there are times when out burdens are so heavy that we have not the strength to roll or drag them; that is when we seek out a prayer partner, a Christian to stand in agreement and believe with us, that what we ask, believing that we have already received, will materialize according to our Faith in the Word of God.

Peter wrote, "Casting the whole of your cares {all you anxieties, all your worries. All your concerns, once and for all} on Him; for He cares for you affectionately and cares about you watchfully" (1 Pet. 5.7 Amp. Bible). This is saying a lot about our New Testament Covenant; how God is available and willing to accept our burdens as His own and either help us to carry them or eliminate them altogether. Prayer is the key to getting supernatural help in this natural world; having God in our world when the world is more or less God-less. Jesus affirmed this when speaking to the disciples concerning the Battle of Life: "Therefore I say to you, do not worry about your life, what you will eat; or about your body, what you will wear. But seek His kingdom, and these things will be given to you as well" (Lk. 12.22,31). Knowing this truth frees us from the anxiety of worrying about finances, health, marriage and the host of other concerns we have as human being living in a materialistic world. God knows that we don't live in a cave; He knows we need a certain amount of money to survive on, and so He says commit our ways to Him and he will take care of us.

Praying In Tongues "For he that speaks in an unknown tongue, speaks not unto men, but unto God; for no man understands him, howbeit in the Spirit he speaks mysteries. 1 "But you, beloved, building up yourself on your most holy faith, praying in the Holy Ghost" ---1 Cor. 14.4; Jude 1.20.

Praying in Tongues is the last type of prayer to be discussed in this chapter. This phenomenon is strictly a New Testament manifestation of the Holy Spirit. Over the years there has been much controversy concerning the Baptism in/with the Holy Spirit, accompanied by the scriptural evidence of speaking in other/ unknown tongues (Acts.2.4).

The Baptism in the Holy Spirit is a second work of Grace through Faith. It was made possible for Believers to receive this gift on the day of Pentecost---fifty days after the crucifixion of the Lord Jesus Christ. Further evidence that we have been Baptized in the Holy Spirit is the manifestation of one or several of the nine Spiritual Gifts: Tongues, Interpretation of Tongues, Discerning of Spirits, Prophecy, Word of Wisdom, Word of Knowledge, Gifts of Healing, Working of Miracles, and the Gift of Faith (1 Cor. 12.7-11).

The difference between the Baptism in the Holy Spirit and Salvation, is that Salvation/Regeneration involves the indwelling and residence of the Holy Spirit within our human spirit causing a spiritual awakening and Eternal Life; whereas, the Baptism in the Holy Spirit is power for service. We can be Saved without the Baptism in the Holy Spirit; but we cannot be un-Saved and Baptized in the Holy Spirit. In order to qualify to receive the second work of Grace, the first work of Grace, Salvation must be accomplished. There are many New Testament examples where the Believer received both apparently at the same time; but in the Word of God, Salvation took first place even if it was only by a second. The manifestations of Spiritual Gifts is not a sign of biblical knowledge, integrity, good character, morals or superiority; it is only that God--- who is no respecter of persons---chose us as a vessel to accomplish some task for Him; and He did the choosing before the foundation of the world.

The benefits to those of us Christians who are Baptized in the Holy Spirit is our increased power and awareness of who we are in Christ, and our ability to talk to the Father, Son or Holy Spirit, and speak mysteries into the natural world, in a language that cannot be twisted or corrupted by our flesh, unclean spirits that may be hidden deep within our soul (intellect, emotions, will, imagination), or those assigned to curse, hinder, tempt, destroy or monitor us. Unclean spirits can create delusions and a blocking action to keep us from asking or receiving the help of God.

They can deceive us into thinking that we are okay, and the Word concerning the renewing of the mind is for other Christians who need it more than we do, that everyone else is wrong; it also can be we are led to believe that no one will ever discover what we are doing. But praying in the Spirit is supernatural and the territorial spirits or indwelling spirits don't know what we are praying about (they lost their ability to interpret this spiritual language). But in our daily dialect---since demons have been on the earth prior to the Garden of Eden---they can understand and fluently speak every language that was ever spoken on earth; but they cannot interpret the Language of the Spirit of Life, the "original" language of God and the holy angels.

Apostle Paul and Apostle Jude wrote that speaking in tongues edifies, builds us up spiritually (1 Cor. 14.4 Jude 1.20). There is yoke-destroying, devil-stomping power in praying in Tongues. "For if I pray in an unknown tongue, my spirit prays, but my understanding is unfruitful" (1 Cor. 14.14). This states that we are strengthened and build up where we are weak, but this is done independently of the intellect, emotions, will and imagination; it cannot be influenced by us or the demonic powers. This is available power for living in Christ. The speaking in Tongues is the Holy Spirit talking or praying from His residence in us. And though we are Saved without this Baptism, and have the Person of the Holy Spirit in us, He has not been given our permission to use our mouth to speak into our life, and to speak the perfect will of God into the earth. We gave Him permission to indwell us and live, but not permission to speak out of our mouth the perfect will of God as He deems (not us) necessary, and at His appropriate timing. This is something to seriously think about!

The Baptism in the Holy Spirit is vital to getting set free on the inside and outside---declaring the Word of God, decreeing the Word of God, and taking spiritual authority through the Word of God by praying in the Holy Spirit. The Baptism in the Holy Spirit tongues can also be prayed corporately, that is, the entire church can pray aloud together (This is not preaching in Tongues which is forbidden because no one knows what is being said); or the Gift of Tongues can be uttered as long as someone immediately interprets it (1 Cor. 14). The Baptism in the Holy Spirit is a must for Christians to fight a winning Battle of Life and For Life.

How do we as Christians get Baptized in the Holy Spirit? Here is a clue:

John the Baptist declared: "But He that sent me to baptize with water, the same said unto me. Upon whom you shall see the Spirit descending, and remain on Him, the same is He which baptizes with the Holy Ghost" (Jn. 1.33). So we see through scriptural reference, the Person John was referring to is Jesus Christ; He is the One who Baptizes us in the Holy Spirit, for He is also the one who sent the Holy Spirit back to the natural realm to continue His work of Redemption.

The Baptism in the Holy Spirit, a gift received by Faith, can be received by direct prayer or laying on of hands by any Christian who is also Baptized in the Holy Spirit. Often, after Inner Healing and Deliverance has taken place, the Baptism in the Holy Spirit is easier to receive.

Deliverance Prayer

Heavenly Father, I humble myself before You in the Name of Jesus Christ. I confess my sins; I am sorry for every one of them. I have accepted Jesus Christ as my Lord and Savior. I am redeemed by the Blood of Jesus and accept Forgiveness Inner Healing and Deliverance. Lord, through the power of the Holy Spirit, completely cleanse me. I have unwisely allowed (Name the unclean spirit(s) to gain access, oppress, torment and use me.

I seek to recover my freedom, wholeness, and to exercise free will over my spirit, soul, mental facilities, will, intellect, emotions, imagination and physical body, to be set free of all infirmities and influences of unclean spirits. I denounce Satan and his plans, purposes, and pursuits. I separate myself from Satan and claim refuge in the Lord Jesus Christ.

I demand and decree my immediate release from all evil spirits and influences operating in my life. In Jesus' Name, I exercise my will and Christian Authority over evil spirits assigned to harass, steal, kill and destroy me. I bind and break your power, strongholds, thinking distortions, delusions, addictions and influences in the Name of Jesus.

BY NOW FAITH: In the Name of Jesus Christ, I NOW declare that you unclean spirits are unlawfully encroaching according to the Word of God: I demand that you leave me! I am a child of God. I declare: Depart from me you cursed spirits!

BY NOW FAITH: I claim the promises: (Joel 2.32) "That whosoever shall call upon the Name of the Lord shall be delivered." The Word cleanses me from all sin. I am a holy temple of God; and Greater is He within me than he that is in the world. I belong to Christ and Him only will I serve.

NOW, I accept my Deliverance. Fill me, Lord, with your Holy Spirit. Bless the Name of Jesus. Amen!

Prayer Of Dominion

Father, in the Name of Jesus, I take spiritual authority against the Principalities, Powers, Rulers of the Darkness and Spiritual Wickedness in the heavenly places assigned to this region. I exercise dominion against all demonic manipulations, control, influences and strongholds. I declare them to be unlawfully assembled according to the Word of God.

Therefore in the Name and by the Blood of Jesus, I render their works bound in the earth as they are in Heaven. In Jesus' Name, I openly declare that every manifestation, operation, assignment or maneuver of the enemy has become ineffective and made void. I exercise dominion against all evil spirits assigned to steal, kill and destroy this people.

In the Name and by the Blood of Jesus Christ, I bind all unclean spirits, including tormenting, perversion, lying, prejudice, racism, anger, hatred, unforgiveness, rebellion, religion, legalism, condemnation, guilt, inferiority, rejection, greed, drug dealing, drug and alcohol addictions, violence, child abuse, domestic violence, pornography, sexual perversions, sin, sicknesses, diseases, poverty--- plus every spirit that binds and oppresses this people.

BY NOW FAITH, I activate the Blood of Jesus over this region and over this people. I declare the Blood to be a witness against the territorial spirit activity and their eternal defeat. I now release this people in the Name of Jesus from all bondages and pronounce them free to serve the Lord Jesus Christ.

BY NOW FAITH, I declare the people blessed and open to the Spirit of God, sensitive to the voice of the Holy Spirit, the Word and the will of God. I decree that where sin abounds that Grace much more abounds, that the Life and Light of Christ prevails against the darkness of Satan, that truth prevails against deception; Deliverance prevails against bondage, and obedience prevails against rebellion. Father, I thank and praise You that Your Kingdom has come and Your will is being done in the earth as it is in Heaven.

I declare in the Name of Jesus that this region is holy ground and consecrated to Your purpose. Holy Spirit, fall upon this region and make Your Presence known, that the will of God be enforced by the Church. To Jesus be honor and glory forever, amen.

Time-Wasters & Haters

"And he shall speak great words against the Most High, and shall ware out the saints of the Most High"--- Dan. 7.25.

These are undoubtedly the years of Restitution and New Beginnings. Those who embrace this paradigm shift that has taken place in the Spirit Realm must be particularly careful as not to allow the enemy to steal our time! We all, being mortals, have a certain amount of time to live, and therefore a limited amount of time to do what God has called us to do.

Satan and the territorial spirits will attempt to persuade us to invest our limited time and resources in the sensual world of pleasure, entertainment and other worldly endeavors, and not be Born Again, or enter into our appointed destiny, and subsequently not finish the course with joy. Time is our valuable asset; seasons are window opportunities placed in time.

If we miss the time we also miss the season. Satan's end-time strategy is to wear out the saints of God. Since he was defeated by Jesus Christ at Calvary, his strategy is to mentally and physically wear us out through futile behaviors, wasted motions and fleshly acts of service---be they religious or secular. The motive is to scatter our attention from the true plan and purpose of God in our life and waste precious time, whereby we leave out of this world tired, worn out, disappointed, disgusted, unsatisfied and defeated.

Time Wasters are demon spirits that hate us and use people to impede out spiritual progress; they but they create and operate through distractions. Distractions manifest as people, events, situations and circumstances that take our focus off of Christ, the Christian Purpose and destiny that God has predestined, prepared and appointed us for.

In the **Battle For Life**, we have to be careful if we are to acquire and maintain our Inner Healing and Deliverance; there are haters among us---servants of the Time-Wasting spirits. Even in the local churches are many Haters; we all know this group or class of Christian---people who don't want to see us prosper. If it were advantageous to plan a Hater's Convention, the extraordinary task would be to find a building large enough to hold so many Haters; or perhaps a large island should be leased? Then, there is always the possibility that no one would come to the Hater's Convention because they hate each other too!

The Haters are the Christian Soldiers who shoot to death their own wounded comrades; who will not lift a finger to support a fallen brother, sister or pastor, but are quick to stand over us and administer the coup de grace. Beware of them: They are one of the most lethal weapons in Satan's arsenal. When we are enjoying our peace and recovery from drugs, alcohol or a sexual morality fall, here they come to forever hold our failure (s) over our head, saying "I am so disappointed in you---how could you have done such a thing! I will never trust you again!" They are Time Wasters.

Other examples of Time Wasters are **Excessive** conventions, board meetings, committees, office parties, sororities, frats, lodges, clubs, functions, toxic relationships, soul ties, arguing, procrastination, family dysfunctions, church programs, drifting from church-to-church, compulsive prophecy hunting, reliving past traumas, all grudges, isolation, rebellion against church leaders, talking, gossip, eating, recreation, vacations, entertainment, social networks, video games, workaholic, love of the world, money, gambling, alcohol, drugs, all sexual immorality, politics for power, non-Christian conventions and meetings, all practicing of non-Christian doctrines, societies (like Eastern Star Masons) and philosophies, avoiding Christian Counseling or Inner Healing & Deliverance when needed.

There are endless ways to waste our precious time here on earth. A cause that appears on the surface to be good, necessary and noble, could actually tie us up and keep us from being used by God, when the position could be adequately filled by someone who doesn't want to serve God. Sometimes, a spirit of "false burden" leads us (deceives us by playing on our emotions, feelings or sense of wanting to see change) to believe that no one can do the job but us; we must sit on the committee at the school board, hospital, city council or even a church-run board.

But if after consulting God we do not receive the "go"---leave it alone; for us, it is a Time Waster, though it may be a legitimate cause and worthy of being done---but not by us! We must redeem the times because the days are extremely evil.

The Undiscovered Country

The Undiscovered Country is similar to the new world that the Europeans arrive in during the 1600s. They risked their lives to venture to the new world, and many of them were buried during the harsh winter. But as soon as the winter was over, they pressed further inland to discover the rest of the country. The Undiscovered Country is that territory within us that we have not known, neither have we explored; for we have not come this way before. The Undiscovered Country is also the New Creature in Christ Jesus, the part of us whom we have to be acquainted with, embrace, love, obey and appreciate, though we know a whole lot about the old creature.

Many philosophers have expounded on this concept by proclaiming, "Know Thyself! Some refer to the old creature we were as the dark side of the soul, or the part of all of us we keep hidden out of sight, suppressed and under lock and key, less he gets out publicly and ruins our entire life. And so, we wear all types of masks and costumes because life is a Broadway production. Therefore, in order to know thyself we have to study thyself in light of what the Word of God says.

The Undiscovered Country is the part of us that if there was no law or punishment for wrongdoing, we would do almost anything! It is our deepest, darkest, best-kept secrets that if anyone found out, they would be appalled. It is that part of us that even God said was desperately wicked. In counseling those incarcerated in prison, it was discovered that the majority of those convicted of heinous crimes including serial murders, never thought that they were capable of such acts.

Even their family members, neighbors and school teachers were shocked to hear of the news. "He is so polite!" Some said, "He is so quiet!" Others said. "He was in church every Sunday," The pastor added. But, of course, they were wrong about what was in that person's heart. We should never say what we will not do; if it were not for the Grace of God that we are in our right mind (some of us) we would be in prison, a mental institution, homeless or on Death Row with the hundreds of men and women exhausting appeals or awaiting execution.

And so it is with the Christians who have fallen. What is needed most is we that are spiritual to help them get back on their feet---not to constantly remind them of the fall, and burn the forever brand on the forehead: SINNER! And more often than not the church aligns in agreement with the world and not the Word of God concerning Repentance and Faith. The world does not believe that fallen people can permanently change because repentance or the "Born Again" experience. It is interesting how certain Christians, the Haters believe that the Blood of Jesus Christ is capable of taking away their sins but not anyone else's sins. It is the double standard in the local church. This type of thinking devalues the Blood of Jesus, and groups it with other religious "phrases".

When we ask a Christian, "How are you doing?" The usual response is, "Blessed." Which is eternally true, but doesn't provide us any useful information to get to know them. They are wearing the "Christian Mask," pretending that they have no problems, struggles, or need prayer or wise counsel for anything.

The devaluing of the power of the Blood causes us to discount the Blood as Atonement for sins of the fallen Christian. The exercise of Faith necessary to invoke the release of cleansing, does not happen because the Blood of Jesus has become a mental and religious concept, and not a Faith-based reality. Therefore, many churches have stopped singing songs about the Blood of Jesus because it sounds gross to them (the Blood being made common as human or animal blood).

So when Christians fall, the response is ridicule, separation or excommunication, "silencing" as the Baptists call it. But God, who knows and is the Way, Truth, and Life said: "The heart is deceitful above all things, and it is exceedingly perverse and corrupt and severely, mortally sick! Who can know it {perceive, understand, be acquainted with his own heart and mind}"---Jer. 19.9. The King

James Version describes the heart as "desperately wicked." The idea is the same: Without the Grace and help of God we might do anything!

The Undiscovered Country is also the place where demonic spirits hide. They hide here because it is the least likely place for us to perceive or be aware of their presence. From the comfortable council room, they pull the strings that make us jump and do weird things---that please them. So, we have to be aware of Seemingly Unimportant Decisions (SUD). When we are not using our minds, being passive or practicing Transcendental Meditation, Yoga, or other Eastern "enlightening" disciplines, we are more open to suggestions than we were if we were using the functions of our mind. When we empty the mind of relevant thoughts and feelings, or cease to monitor our thoughts, feelings and emotions, we enter into the Undiscovered Country. And like the "default" setting and subprogram on a computer that returns when it has lost track of what it is doing, we return and lean on the familiar arm of the flesh; there, the demons are waiting to get control of our life; and the SUD thought is likely the one that leads us in the direction to sin; because it will be the one that come out of us so powerfully; nevertheless, we will know it for what it is because it will NEVER pass the test of the Word of God!

Many people have fallen into sin because of that Seemingly Unimportant Decision. It could be visiting an ex-girlfriend when one or both people are married; or going to the store in the middle of the night and get robbed! On that note, thousands of people are in prison because of the sudden urge to go someplace or do something uncharacteristic of them and weird.

Vain Imaginations

"Casting down imaginations...and bringing into captivity every thought to the obedience of Christ"---2Cor. 10.5.

Thoughts + Feelings +Emotions = Behaviors. As stated earlier, there is such a thing as the imagination being out of phase with the rest of the mind, including the intellect. A Christian must guard against recurring thoughts that belong to the old man or demons, who will use these thoughts to regain his former position; and the spirits that are associated with the old man will definitely use the flesh, the self-life and the Law of Sin and Death to regain control.

Demonic Interference

Although there are hundreds of symptoms of demonic interference, some of which have their root in emotional and medical disorders that may be chemical or electrical related, a physician should always be consulted. As these lists are only a guide-line to recognizing problems, it is not meant to be conclusive or a substitute for medical attention.

Fail to get breakthrough after days of fasting and prayers. Unexplained illness with no diagnosis, including rashes. Practicing the Occult (including witchcraft, Tara Cards, Voodoo and Ouija board). Repeated backsliding in the same area. Chronic depression, suicide attempts, hostile behavior, unexplained sulfur-like odor, seizures, suddenly compelled to go places, cutting the flesh, excessive compulsive behaviors, difficulty reading Bible, difficulty worshipping, difficulty repenting, mental illnesses (all types), hearing voices, mocking the Word of God, cursing God or Jesus, superhuman strength, terror in the mind, recurring nightmares, flashbacks, seeing evil spirits, claims to be a reincarnation, actual visitation by evil spirits.

Jesus is the Great Physician. He said, "Ask and you shall receive. It is always to our best interest to do what Jesus says. But often times, we find it all but impossible to obey His Word. These are times when the influences of the demonic kingdom, family, friends and religious folks are at their worst in our lives. It is beneficial to our spiritual growth to be find a trusted, dedicated, non-judgmental professional to get help; a ministry empowered by the Holy Spirit and devoted to setting the captives free, is what's needed; not a gossiper or busybody. We should pray and ask God to direct us to someone whom He uses to release and activate Physical Healing, Emotional Healing, Deliverance and Restoration.

Why do you seek Healing & Deliverance?

We as Christians are required to live by the Standard of the Word of God. The Christian denominations, the Constitution and legal system even adds a little more to that. Christians are to live a life above reproach and blame. Many of us strive daily to live up to these standards; sometimes we are trusting in God, other times we are maintaining a façade, the appearance of living holy---going through the motions---when in fact we are only suppressing the manifestations of our urges, fantasies and desires. But even the smallest volcano will someday blow, and the destruction in its wake can be most devastating to those around it.

The Undiscovered Country is full of active and dormant volcanoes: Some small and others humongous. Many have erupted and spent their fury and now lain dormant. But there are many more potential disasters lurking deep below the surface. Under the right conditions they will bust loose with a fury that would be impossible for us to contain; impatience turns into irritation; irritation into anger; anger into rage; rage into violence; violence into murder; murder into imprisonment; imprisonment into State Execution.

Secret sins are not volcanoes but the effect are the same. Those urges that we suppress, fail to suppress and indulge in behind closed doors will be discovered.

Below are a few "volcanoes" and manifestations of demonic activity. Some are already listed in the other categories: Fear, worry, sickness and disease, chronic pain, Crack/cocaine/heroin, prescription drug addiction, Marijuana, cigarettes, psychological addictions, gambling, rejection, rebellion, guilt, shame, pride stress, bitterness, jealousy, violence, road rage, criminality, stealing;

Overeating, laziness, procrastination, cursing, suicide, self hatred, lust abandonment, depression, obsession, emotional abuse, physical abuse, sexual abuse, incest, abortion, fornication, adultery, pornography, homosexuality, Lesbianism, Pedophilia, masturbation, fetishes, necrophilia, bestiality, forgetfulness, curses, hearing voices mental illness, paranoia, hatred of men, hatred of women, spousal abuse, witchcraft, demonic interference, cults, religious error, can't find or keep employment, problems concentrating, can't solve simple problems.

The Undiscovered Country can be a very crowded place, a place that we seldom visit to clean house, but the occupants seem to come and go as they please! This is the place the Holy Spirit goes in and cleans house; He heals the hurts and soothes the pains; this is where He restores the fractured or fragmented personality---having been wounded during the Battle of Life and **The Battle For Life**.

Our personality was fractured by our own sins and lifestyle plus the deeds of familiar and territorial spirits. This was also added to by family and social pressures, abuse and betrayals; this is where the Love of Christ rushes in like a mighty wind and sweeps away the entrenched spirits who have been dictating to us their will and sometimes even our will---because, at times, we enjoyed sinning! Even in a court of law, "the devil made me do it," Is not an accepted defense! We are responsible to God for the vain imaginations that lead us into actions that jeopardize our entire being; spirit, soul, natural body, and freedom, even though we may have been coerced.

U.S. Prison Population Tops 2 Million

America's prison population topped 2 million inmates for the first time in history on June 30, 2002 according to a new report from the Justice Department's Bureau of Justice Statistics (BJS). The 50 states, the District of Columbia and the federal government held 1,355,748 prisoners (two-thirds of the total incarcerated population), and local municipal and county jails held 665,475 inmates.

By midyear 2002, America's jails held 1 in every 142 U.S. residents. Males were incarcerated at the rate of 1,309 inmates per 100,000 U.S. men, while the female incarceration rate was 113 per 100,000 women residents. Of the 1,200,203 state prisoners, 3,055 were younger than 18 years old. In addition, adult jails held 7,248 inmates under 18. State and federal correctional authorities held 88,776 non-citizens. And a conservative estimate of those incarcerated worldwide is 9 million souls; this includes the innocent, persecuted Christians, political prisoners and mental institutions to "quiet the opposition." America leads the world in freedoms, but also leads the world in criminals.

The legacy of the true Christian is not we never fall, but if we fall we have Jesus Christ to help us get back up. Many Heavy Weight Boxing champions have been knocked down, only to return in the later rounds to win. So it is with us; we may be down at times but we get back up before the bell rings and the fight is over.

Inner Healing takes place when we pour out our heart to God; we empty ourselves of our own plans, hopes, ambitions, pride and self-sufficiency and ask God to search our entire heart, the deepest recesses and territory within the Undiscovered Country, to bind up our broken heart and comfort our morning, and provide the oil of gladness, a garment of praise instead of the spirit of discouragement and despair; to drive out the enemy and set fire to his camp---the fire of the Holy Ghost---and set us at liberty, who have been bruised.

The healing of past hurts and bruised emotions will effect a lasting change in the way we think. The renewing of the mind and the balancing of the intellect, emotions, will and imagination will also happen; the removal of unclean spirits, strongholds, delusions, vain imaginations, thinking distortions and the territorial spirit control that we believed as truth will be revealed for what they are---lies! Before we know it, the mind will quiet and have less background chatter going on (demons are gone, no more board meetings). And we will be able to sleep soundly, awaken refreshed, and have a closer, intimate relationship with God.

To Know Christ: The word "know" in biblical sense means a lot more than a casual acquaintance or intellectual knowledge of someone or something. To know, for example in Adam's or Abraham's case, meant to have sexual relations with, to also be legally married to that person; apart from the biblical use of "laid with," which implies sexual union without the benefits of marriage, and thus the Blessing of God that accompanies holy matrimony isn't present; the latter is sin and a negative soul-tie. Therefore to know Christ is more than going to Church, preaching, teaching, singing, ushering, board membership, tithing and all the other important functions that make up the local churches; but knowing Christ apart from services, programs, duties and people.

We desire to have these open lines of communication but someone or something keeps getting in our way. We feel the power of His Presence while the praise and worship music is playing, during the preaching and prayer line, but as soon as we leave, it's as though God lives in the brick and mortar building but not in us; or, the Anointing stays with us for a while then fades like the perfume or cologne we strategically applied at 8:00 a.m. in the morning but now it's 10:00 p.m. and dark outside.

Fading glory isn't what God desires for us; ever-increased glory is what He wants; and we will have what we say. The reason that we experience the tremendous power of God while in the Church building is the Corporate Anointing. Jesus said that where two or three are gathered together in His Name that He would be in the midst of them. It is equally true that an intercessory-prayer-strengthened Corporate Anointing blocks out the overhead local demonic powers that interfere in our lives via mental oppression, suggestions and phobias. Another reason why we cannot experience Christ in us is the presence of demonic spirits in our soul or physical body; these evil entities may be silenced, made ineffective while we're in the Presence of Christ and His Anointing, but revive and function when we leave the Church and His Corporate Presence. Religious spirits of tradition, legalism or formalism could be present but silenced during the service; they are spirits that deceive us to believe that Sunday morning Church is good, in that it also makes us look and feel good about ourselves; it's all that's needed for spiritual maturity, and all that God requires of us as devote Christians. So the rest of the week is ours, unless we decide to attend an optional Bible Study and Prayer meeting.

But, then again, we can't blame Satan for everything. Still another reason is that our flesh isn't under the complete control of our human spirit who is indwelled and being led by the Holy Spirit; there's a part that's still "us", and not conformed to the image of Jesus Christ. What percentage of Christ verses us---90-10, 70-30, 50-50, 20-80 etc., decides who's in control of our life. The lower the percentage of Christ-control in us, the easier it is to return to our old self-life and our scandalous ways.

As Christians we received the Holy Spirit as a complete Person: 100%. We didn't receive a "part" or "piece" of Him; but we do have control over how much He effects change in us. In general, sin has attached to it a pleasure principle; if sin always brought excruciating pain every time, no one but the most hard core sadist would have anything to do with it. Because sin is pleasurable, the body and mind remembers it well, and tried to return to it every chance it gets.

If the mind of the flesh (or lust of the flesh), as the Word describes this principle, reasons on a non-spiritual (assisted by Christ) but religious level that to be a good Christian it is wrong to participate in certain sin, it will counter-reason and subconsciously seek another outlet to express its desires.

For example: you may stop drinking alcohol and have years of "clean time" and you did it because it's the Christian thing to do, but now you occasionally visit a phonographic website to view naked women/men; or a chat line to talk to single women when we are married and our wife is asleep in the bedroom, then we have only exchanged one sin for another, and not been set free.

Nevertheless, if we are determined to know Christ in us, there is a lot to overcome in this world. God told Jeremiah and it also applies to us: "Call upon Me, and I will answer you" (Jer. 33:3). In this century of technology: Satellites, Internet, social networks, electronics, Voice Mail and E-Mail, it's relatively easy to contact people providing they want to be contacted! But none of it will help us contact God.

This is because God communicates at a different level, and has different means of communication. He often uses the "inner" channel; it's His private line. Not only can God communicate, but He has promised in His Word to answer us if we by faith call upon the Name of Jesus. This alone expresses His will towards us: He is able and willing to help! He said, "Ask, and you shall receive, that your joy may be full" (Jn. 16:24). What we confess with our mouth is also important to what our experience in Christ becomes. The Word in Romans 10:9 says, "If you will confess with your mouth the Lord Jesus, and believe in your heart that God raised Him from the dead, you will be saved."

In the same way that faith is important to receive Salvation, faith is equally important to receive physical healing or spiritual deliverance from the oppression of indwelling evil spirits. A vocal confession establishes in the earth what is believed [adhered to, trusted in and relied on] in the heart. There are two biblical Confessions: The Confession of sin and the Confession of Faith; both are needed in the entire Christian journey.

After Salvation, the Confession of sin only applies when we sin after accepting Jesus as Savior and Lord (Jn.3:16). But the Confession of Faith is needed to receive from God what's needed in our life and the lives of others; this includes Deliverance. It is necessary to pray and speak the Word of God to specifically target indwelling or familiar spirits in our life. Jesus sent His Word to deliver us from bondage; it is for freedom that Christ has set us free. Let's look at Joshua and how he obtained the Promise: "Every place where your foot shall step, I have given it to you for an inheritance" (Josh. 1:3). This Word of Promise was given to Joshua and the Children of Israel to stir up their faith in the God, Jehovah--whom the majority of the Israelites didn't know, because they were too young to remember the former attempt by their parents.

Their parents, because of their unbelief and a lack of faith, failed to obtain their inheritance. God was telling this group that faith is a possessor of the promises of God, that they should focus their minds and hearts upon Him who is their Source —for the battle isn't theirs but the Lord's. God encouraged them; He motivated them to believe His words as though the Promised Land was already theirs----which spiritually (by faith) it already was!

They were raised up for such a time as this to be conquerors, to take by the force of faith the Promise that God made. Even today, we as Christians are to by Faith, take possession of the promises of God that have been written in the Word of God and purchased by the Blood of Jesus Christ. We are to press in and take by the Spirit what the Word of God generously states belongs to us; by the violence of the Holy Spirit, we are to by faith take our healing, deliverance, peace, joy, finances, etc., from the clutches and stranglehold of the devil!

We drive out the Anakims of unbelief and fear---spirits who have come between us and our covenant rights. And we do not stop until our life and our love ones are completely taken over-taken by the blessings of God by Jesus Christ."For we wrestle not against flesh and blood, but against principalities, against powers, against the rulers of the darkness of this world, against spiritual wickedness in the high places" (Eph. 6:12).

Does every Believer in Jesus Christ need Inner Healing? The answer to that question is Yes! As the above scripture indicates, there is a controlling demonic government reigning and ruling over the residents of the physical world. The descendents of Adam and Eve who are born into this world are under the curse of the Mosaic Law (except Jesus of Nazareth, the Christ).

We are born in sin, spiritually dead, and therefore subject to the ruler of this world---Satan. Everyone, Christian or non- Christian are exposed to the controlling and manipulative influence of these principalities, powers, rulers, and high-seated personalities on a daily basis. These demonic spirits began influencing and forming our thought patterns, by way of activating generational curses, creating mental and physical strongholds and bondages before we are born; in the womb spirits of rejection and fear are often imparted by way of the parent's attitude towards the unborn child. Even the best of parents are only human, and subject to impart by way of oral instruction, discipline, lifestyle, or association, the wisdom accum-ulated in and of this world which is demonic and self-destructive.

It is certain that the worst of parents will impose his or her beliefs, attitudes, prejudices, habits or worldly standards on their children. Associations and soul ties at school, work, fiats, lodges, fornication, media, music lyrics and people with toxic personalities add to the need to receive Jesus Christ's His Inner Healing and Deliverance.

When we accept Jesus Christ as our personal Lord and Savior, the Holy Spirit indwells our human spirit and causes us to be spiritually alive. The presence of the Holy Spirit establishes ownership, and thus the process of Sanctification commences: We are set apart to serve God; it also includes Inner Healing and Deliverance, to conforms us into the image of Jesus Christ by the renewing of the mind, healing of emotional trauma, instruction in the Word of God—thus countering the lie, the breaking of curses and the ejecting of demonic spirits.

Inner Healing and Deliverance is necessary because we also have a soul body (intellect, emotions, and will) and a physical body also. Within these two parts of the whole (spirit body, soul body, physical body), the need to uncover and address the hidden root causes of infirmity are necessary. This is accomplished by dealing with the mental processes, behaviors, practices, curses, soul ties, emotions, disobedience, parental relationship, sexual sin, strongholds, bondages, addictions and places of frequent visitation have to be addressed and reconciled by way of the cross of Jesus Christ.

These things must suffer death, so that the life of Christ and the effectual power of His resurrected life and the truth will have His way not only where He dwells in the spirit body, but also in the soul and physical body. Then He can bring healing and deliverance to the entire person; and use that person to touch the lives of others in the Body of Christ and the world. As Sanctification is a lifelong process, so is Inner healing and Deliverance. Because the average Christian has experienced many years of "world programming", it doesn't suddenly disappear in a few hours of an Inner Healing and Deliverance session. In the same manner that we are instructed to work out our own salvation, we are to do the same in our getting set free from the contamination of the world.

CHAPTER FIVE

Forgiveness Brings Healing

"And when you stand praying, forgive ...That your Father also which is in heaven may forgive your trespasses. 26 But if you do not forgive, neither will your Father forgive your trespasses"---Mk. 11.25,26.

"Then said Jesus, Father forgive them; for they know not what they do" (Lk. 23:34).

Jesus spoke these immortal words as He hung bleeding and dying upon the cross. As He hung suspended between Heaven and earth, *Jesus* asked His Father to forgive the Jews and Romans for nailing His hands and feet to the cross, and forgive those who despised and hated Him without a real cause. His whole life had been one supreme sacrifice, a life of miracles, signs and wonders.

From His incarnation to the cross, was the fulfillment of the Father's plan to grant forgiveness of sins through a one-time offering; by the shedding of His Son's blood, Jehovah-Elohim would accept it as Atonement for the sins of mankind. Jesus declared: "It is finished!" After He spoke these word He released His Spirit. A Roman officer and several soldiers struck their chests; they were glad this task was over with.

These men had executed hundreds of criminals, and with all of them the suffering and death was usually the same. Yet--with Jesus, the officer concluded that, "Truly this was the Son of God" (Mt. 27:54). He came to this conclusion because no one he had previously executed had ever forgave those who put them through such a agonizing death.

Crucifixion was a suffocating death. Jesus was whipped to weaken His body; His hands and feet were tied to the cross with rope, then nailed to the cross; the cross was stood up and dropped into a hole in the ground; the sudden jolt began the process. The crucifixion of Jesus weakened His physical body; He struggled to remain erect; His breathing becomes erratic when His chest muscles spasm, shock set in and the muscles and lungs collapsed. Usually the legs of the man were broken to speed up the process, as not to allow the man to continuously push himself up to grasp for air, and thus prolonging the inevitable; but Jesus' legs weren't broken because He expired early. In the eyes of these Romans, it wasn't humanly possible to be so forgiving, good and com-passionate---unless Jesus was, as He claimed, the Son of God. His words of forgiveness convinced them.

The foundation principle of Salvation is forgiveness; the New Testament Covenant we have with God is also based on forgiveness. Forgiveness was a decision God made in His eternal counsels before the foundation of the world. He made the decision not to exert His legal right---He surrendered His right to retribution, His right to retaliate for the wrongs that He received through Adam's treason and the disobedience of his descendents.

As forgiveness is an act of God's will, so it's also an act of our will. As we put on Christ and become a new creature our human spirit has already been resurrected, yet our soul and mental facilities are being renewed day by day. In this renewal comes a different way of thinking, a new way of negotiating our way through the trials and tribulations of dealing with people. The old man, the old ways of doing and dealing with life must be crucified; what we used to call "justice" was most likely revenge in disguise. We cannot study Forgiveness without also studying Unforgiveness.

Harboring a spirit or attitude of Unforgiveness is sin. We are supposed to be liberated from habitual sin, for "whom the Son has set free is free indeed" (Jn. 8:36). Unforgiveness binds us to the former self-life, the Broad Road that leads to destruction. The divine Presence of the Holy Spirit will flow like the Colorado River in and out of our heart as we practice the action---the act of Forgiveness; Forgiveness is an act of love and grace that God ordained to set us free from the past and the need for revenge.

Though it may be easier for God and Jesus to forgive---because They have had more practice---it isn't easy for the average person to forgive. Forgiveness is something learned and then practiced under the guidance of the Holy Spirit, who is God. The more serious the trespasses are against us, the more difficult it is to forgive; but nevertheless, Forgiveness is possible.

Being one with God, the Holy Spirit who permeates the earth and inhabits Believers is the forgiver of sins, and helps us to forgive the trespasses of others; because He inhabits us, He is aware when a person offends us or even offends Him inside us. When someone offends us the Holy Spirit, God, moves to arrange Forgiveness. God doesn't only act from Heaven, but from His position on earth within us.

He looks out of our eyes and hears with our ears what's going on in our life and environment. Jesus asked His Father to forgive His executioners. Why not forgive them Himself? Jesus was completely submitted to His Father, and only spoke and did what His Father told Him to. He was sent into the world by the Father; Jesus was the human Son of His Father. The Father had been wronged by His Son being murdered by the Jews and Romans. Therefore, Jesus asked His Father to forgive them for what they did, not for what they are.

God forgave them and surrendered His right to get even; God acknowledged the pain of His loss, appropriated it to the Plan of Salvation, and went on with His Life. God didn't in any way indorse, tolerate, minimize, excuse or cover up the evil behavior of the mortals, the wrong actions of the Jews and Romans, but simply forgave them according to the multitude of His love, grace, mercy and Forgiveness. Our self-life attitude, the natural man would rather eat glass than to forgive a neighbor who really fouls up. We may pretend or say that we forgive but our attitude and actions towards her shows that we haven't forgiven her.

On a subconscious level the trespass is as fresh as the moment it happened; we avoid her---can't stand being around her. Instead of going to the super market Saturday morning, we switch to Saturday night to avoid her. At church when we used to sit with her, we now sit in a pew on the opposite side of the sanctuary. Obviously we haven't forgiven her. We have not considered that she is human and entitled to Forgiveness by us as part both of our healings and spiritual journey through this land. As spiritual as we may think we are we will someday need a human being to forgive us. Are we willing to forgive, revise our feelings, consider her good points that caused us to like her in the first place?

As a senior citizen, due to our declining memory, strain to remember why we don't like a certain individual or family members. We have held that grudge for so long that we have forgotten the reason and circumstances surrounding the mishap. We may even use the word "hate" to describe our personal feelings towards that person who offended us; but having an unforgiving heart is to have a hateful heart. But we aren't hurting anyone but ourselves, making our own life miserable, while the person that we hate probably can care less how we feel about him, and is enjoying his life to the hilt, while we are marinating in evil and wallowing in hate and victimization.

First: we acknowledge that a wrong has been done to us personally, that is, we have personally suffered emotionally, physically or materially a wrong (an exclusion would be to forgive someone who commits a third-party trespass, that is, a trespass against someone we care for, and it emotionally or in some other way affects us.).

Second: Acknowledge what they did, but separate what they did from who they are as human beings.

Third: Acknowledge our loss, pain or hurt feelings.

 Fourth: Forgive them for what they did, not why they did it. We have now surrendered our right to retaliate, and are set free from the burden of revenge. We do not by forgiving them endorse, tolerate, minimize, excuse and cover up their behavior. Forgiveness frees us from the need to take up for ourselves through retaliation that may lead to violence and more hurt. We appropriate our loss or pain to the unfairness of living in a sin-cursed world, and leave it at that; we wish the person the best in life and leave it at that. There's no way to actually change the past; not even God changes the past, nor does He even want to.

Forgiveness rises up out of our spirit, giving us the desire to settle the matter in a righteous way. This desire, if heeded, will cause the pent-up emotions inside us that are holding us as debtor in debtor's prison to be released; the Spirit of God working through our spirit will heal the hurt and open the prison door; the prison of Unforgiveness, like a stone wall, separates us from God; that stone wall must fall, and become a bridge for our feet to walk over the troubled waters of life. Unforgiveness is non-spiritual drudgery. When we're set free from Unforgiveness, a serious blockage has been removed, a stumbling block to our spiritual growth.

Many times the Baptism in the Holy Spirit and Spiritual Gifts have been known to come through with amazing manifestations once Unforgiveness has been dealt with and peace restored in the heart. Unforgiveness is like a demonic dam holding back the living waters of the Holy Spirit; once the dam is detonated, the Curse of Disobedience brought about by hatred is superseded by the Blessings for Obedience.

Criminal Justice

Scriptural Forgiveness doesn't mean that we surrender our rights to the United States Constitution and State Constitution concerning due process, equal protection under the law, access to the Civil and Criminal Justice Systems, and Law Enforcement.

Forgiveness doesn't mean that we have to remain or return to a mentally, physically or sexually abusive relationship; a woman abused by her husband or boyfriend must seek in her heart to forgive him for abusing her, but she's not obligated to stay or return, reunite with him and tolerate the abusive relationship. Forgiveness and Reunion are two different things. Forgiveness on the part of the victim is uncond-itional---it has nothing to do with whether he's sorry for what he's done to her, asks for forgiveness, laughs in her face, or goes to jail for his behavior.

Reunion is conditional that the relationship becomes peaceful, loving and safe. Reunion involves his changed behavior, even participation in Anger Management Counseling, repentance, sorrow and apology, showing himself again trustworthy and nonaggressive. Reunion is sometimes unwise, impractical, and can lead to more abuse or even death. Forgiveness doesn't mean that we are at the mercy of criminals. Yet Forgiveness is a personal process, a personal way to bring healing to the victim, and even to the assailant who may request Forgiveness; so,

Forgiveness isn't designed to clear corporations, organizations, institutions, governments or groups of people from criminal acts or civil litigations.

There have been thousands of crimes against humanity since the Garden of Eden: Genocide, Slavery and Terrorism being only a few---spurring plenty of reasons why the people of the world could hate each other: But how can these atrocities be forgiven? Will God forgive what governments and organizations of wicked peoples have inflicted upon humanity? No! God doesn't "collectively" forgive sins or the deeds of criminal enterprises; **God judges the sins of nations, and personally will forgive individuals—**those who ask for Forgiveness of their personal sins, their part in the crimes; neither are we as human being required or obligated to forgive what these governments and terrorists have done as a group. We can only forgive what has been personally done to us or our love ones; Forgiveness is personal.

Forgiveness is a personal act, of the healing or healed heart. We will live with the knowledge of these tragedies, not hold their descendants and relatives personally responsible, and not retaliate or exclude them from civilization because of what has happened; but we don't have any more right than God wills to forgive them.

People who commit crimes, including foreign combatants, terrorist and other organized criminals should be apprehended and prosecuted, not forgiven; the lawbreakers should be tried in the appropriate court or International Tribunal, and punished to the extent of the law: This is justice, not revenge. God has provided a system to deal with all types of criminals: Yet be very careful:

Many of us are prisoners of what happened to us years ago; we are caught in the Unforgiveness trap, the trap of retaliation and revenge. A terrorists detonates a bomb and kills someone we love(whether domestic or in foreign lands); a drunk driver injures, cripples or kills our child; these things are difficult but not impossible to deal with. A criminal abuses, a teacher sexually molests our child, robs or commits any variety of criminal acts against us or a close member of our family, and it's easy to become bitter, a prisoner doing time in the dungeon of Unforgiveness: and we claim that we want justice---the perpetrator to pay---but deep in our heart it is more revenge than real justice.

It's righteous to demand that a criminal be brought to justice, but this "justice" cannot include knowingly making false statements or false accusations on our part; the legal and righteous judgment of the case cannot be rooted in our personal satisfaction which amounts to revenge. In a civil case justice cannot amount to overvaluing, inflating the damage or loss that would be lying, perjury, greed and revenge being perpetrated by us, a false witness. If we get caught up in wanting someone to pay, in reality that someone will be us. As Christians we have to be careful of our motives.

In America we have a Criminal Justice System. Its function is to identify, prosecute and punish offenders who trample upon the rights of others and break the law. These appointed, paid public servants in the legal system decide the innocence or guilt of the defendant. God had ordained these authorities to govern and provide protection for the innocent. If by chance a defend-ant, though guilty, escapes human justice, he never escapes the Justice of God.

"Vengeance is Mine: I will repay, says the Lord" (Ro. 12:19).

According to the Word, the duty of vengeance doesn't belong to us but to the Lord; our duty of Forgiveness replaces our need for vengeance; God will even the score if that's what's needed to straighten out a criminal trespasser. So if our assailant is found guilty and sentenced to prison, don't rejoice or burden the conscious by hating him also. Forgiveness doesn't mean that we forget what happened but are doing the right thing to bring **CLOSURE** what happened.

It is a known fact that people can change with the help of God; it's also a fact that criminals are people and therefore qualify to change. Remember that Moses, David, and Saul of Tarsus were once murderers! Thousands of incarcerated men and women who have done the most brutal crimes have been saved by the Lord Jesus Christ. The Lord has forgiven them of their entire life of sin---not just what they've done to get into prison.

And though a prisoner has been forgiven by Jesus Christ, it doesn't mean that the consequences, the prison sentence disappears, nor their victim comes back alive, are healed or emotionally set free; the past remains the past and cannot be changed. That is why it is important that we, the survivor forgive, to set ourselves free from the past.

Closure does not imply that everything reverts back to its original state. It is untrue that criminals go to prison, pretend to get saved and are released early; the truth is that the nation's parole boards interview hundreds of former priests, pastors and church officials at their parole hearings; the parole board has no interest in real or pretend religious conversions. The parole board looks at the past criminal history, present crime, prison conduct, psychological reports, and future community placement arrangement. The point being, many offenders truly are saved and lead anointed and fruitful lives—sometimes better Christian lives than those who never went afoul of the law, far better lives than those who visit the prison to minister.

Thousands of offenders have given their lives to the Lord Jesus Christ and have received the Baptism in the Holy Spirit; signs and wonders following as they preach and teach the Word to the other prisoners. God, who isn't a respecter of persons, also pours out His Love, Fruit of the Spirit---character--- and Spiritual Gifts on incarcerated men and women; many of which were already Saved but got in trouble, and God allowed them to be "corrected" in a Correctional Facility of His timing and choosing.

God isn't angry at them for their former crimes, but is well pleased with their present Repentance and Faith. The outside volunteers who weekly visit them bear witness to the greatness of Jesus Christ in the prison system. Again, it is a fact that people can and do change; criminals repent, are converted and become some of the most useful Christians in the Body of Christ. We fail to realize that many of our past and present leaders in the Body of Christ were also ex-convicts, ex-drug pushers, ex-drug addicts, ex-pimps, ex- prostitutes, ex-this and ex-that.

Yet it seems that we dance and shout in church, but when we get personally victimized we forget about what God can do and concentrate on what we can do to that low-life dirt bag---as fugitives are called on a certain national television cop show. Think about this: A man robs us; he's caught, sentenced and goes to prison.

In prison he repents and gets Saved. During his walk with Jesus he produces Fruit consistent with Salvation; he no longer continues in his criminal ways---would we as a Born Again Christian want to see this man kept in prison, bound to his past criminal history after he has received Forgiveness from God, be bound to a past he cannot change? Or should he be given a another chance to redeem himself? An unforgiving person sounds like an actor in a horror movie: The buried corpse of the person who has been murdered, rises from the grave and shrieks, "I want revenge!"

The Prosecutor's Office

It's true---even the unsaved know that we as Christians don't practice what we preach. In minor incidents, we are the first ones in line at the prosecutor's office. Instead of trying to work out our disagreement---the neighbor's dog regularly turns over our garbage cans---we want to show that neighbor (not love) but how tough we are; that we are legally right and the neighbor is wrong, and should be put in his place and his dog put to sleep! Then during our prayer time we have the nerve to utter to God, "Lord, forgive me for my sins!" But you won't forgive our neighbor who trespassed against us!

Prison Without Walls

Throughout America parole boards meet to consider the release of offenders. The majority of these prisoners have served beyond their Minimum Court Sentence. We Christians cannot harbor an unforgiving or hateful spirit towards these offenders. Even after some prisoners have served ten or twenty years, we the victim cannot forgive and go on with our life--- unless we for certain that our assailant is safely locked away forever, and miserable as we are miserable, well beyond what the Sentencing Judge deemed appropriate to fit the crime:

We are in prison with them too; we are their invisible bunk-mates serving the exact sentence given them, but serving it in our homes. We need to be set free through Deliverance and Inner Healing. We Christians have a National Day of Prayer; there ought to be a National Forgiveness Day; the main people that will be set free would be Christians and non-Christians, who have been victimized more by our own unforgiving hearts than what the criminals did to us! As Christians we know that sin is sin; There are no little and big sins for all unrighteousness is sin, and all sin must be repented of.

According to the Word of God, the sin of murder, rape, robbery, lying, fornication, cheating, greed, pride and unforgiveness is the same; any of these sins can land us in Hell. "When the enemy shall come in like a flood, the Spirit of the Lord will lift up a standard against him" (Isa. 59:19). God sets the standard, His way of doing things.

We must always seek to discover that standard and apply it. We cannot be vigilantes, go on our own personal crusade, a vendetta, seeking the justice we think we deserve. If justice is what God sought, then He would've killed us all! Instead His Mercy prevailed and triumphed over Judgment, and He spared us.

The Word also reminds us that "God cast our sins behind His back" (Isa. 38:17). In doing so, "He will not remember our sins" (Isa 43:35). And if that wasn't enough, "As far as the east is from the west, so far has He removed our trespasses from us" (Ps. 103:11).

Obviously, God's not trying to, and goes to great lengths, to forgive and forget our sins, and not rub our sins in our faces, what spiritual criminals we've been, and, in some areas, still are. Having within ourselves the same Spirit, we must of necessity manifest the character fruit of Forgiveness. Or do we pick over the Bible, choosing what part we will or will not do?

Settling Old Accounts

21 "Then came Peter, to Him, and said, Lord how often shall my brother sin against me, and I forgive him? Until seven times? 22 Jesus said... not seven times, until seventy times seven"---Mt. 18.21,22 "Eye for eye, tooth for tooth, hand for hand, foot for foot, burning for burning, wound for wound, stripe for stripe. If an ox gore a man or a woman, that they die; then the ox shall be surely stoned...But if the ox were wont with his horn in the past, and it hath been testified to his owner...the ox shall be stoned, and his owner shall be put to death"---Ex. 21.24-29.

The Mosaic Law was uncompromising in its meter of justice. At an early age, Peter had learned that in the Jewish society there was little consideration for accidents; Forgiveness wasn't written into the Mosaic Law. Jesus came to change that, to fulfill the legal and spiritual requirements of the Law: Jesus wanted Peter and all Believers to live by Grace through faith by obeying His commandments.

Simon Peter had been listening to Jesus for some time now. Peter was an impulsive fellow. Whatever he did was to the extreme. He thought by suggesting seven times to forgive his brother was being generous and spiritual. The Master suggested that Peter's generosity was but legalism in disguise, the focusing on the Letter of the Law and not the Spirit application it.

Jesus answered Peter's hypothetical question with a hypothetical 490 times answer, showing him that Forgiveness wasn't a numbers game--- a so many and no more formula. When the Master finished with Peter, he realized that Forgiveness was an expression of grace; that grace and truth came by Jesus Christ. When Peter calculated that 70x7=490, he thought that it would be more sensible to pack up the wife and children, leave town with no forwarding address than to forgive his brother that many times! But Jesus wasn't teaching about how many times, how long, what types of sins, or how many people involved in a transgression. *Jesus* told Peter to forgive his brother.

We don't know whether Peter's brother actually offended him a lot, but Jesus didn't tell Peter to tolerate, excuse or in any way minimize the wrong that his brother inflicted on him; or that Peter had to continuously be victimized by his brother either psychologically, physically or suffer material lost from thief, damage or misuse. In short, if Peter's brother was living with him Peter could demand that he straighten up or find his own place to live!

Many who quote "an eye for an eye" need to read the rest of the Law of Moses; after reading it in its entirety, would undoubtedly discover that we have missed the mark in another area, and therefore would be guilty of transgressing the entire Law, since no ordinary human being ever keep the requirements of the Law; and today we would not want to live under such stringent regulations.

If Forgiveness was strictly about numbers, God has already forgiven us thousands of times for our sins; it's reasonable to confess that we were habitual sinners, and needed a great God with a habitual forgiving heart: This we have in Jesus Christ. Sometime after we were Saved and filled with the Holy Spirit we forgot how evil we really were; though we shouldn't allow our negative past to interfere, adversely influence our present spiritual and psychological walk with Jesus, nonetheless, we can't keep a running account on our neighbor's character flaws and forget where we came from.

The Forgiveness that we sought and obtained must be applied with the same compassion that Jesus applied to us. In this we need to be more sensitive to the spiritual needs of others, their wrestling with the same demonic spirits that we daily wrestle with; to the end that we may forgive like Jesus forgave us. As we are the temples of the forgiving God, we can choose to exercise His righteousness and forbearance in literally not counting other peoples trespasses against them: "It was God [personally present] in Christ, reconciling and restoring the world to favor with Himself, not counting up and holding against [men] their trespasses [but reconciling them]...(2 Cor. 5:19).

23 "Therefore is the kingdom of heaven likened unto a certain king, which would take account of his servants. 24 And when he had begun to reckon, one was brought unto him, which owed him ten thousand talents (a million dollars)"---Mt. 18.23,24.

Again Jesus taught on the importance of Forgiveness. Forgiveness is the road to healing the past, possible reconciliation, reunion and restoration. Jesus compared Himself to an earthly king who one day settled His old accounts. The servant in question could have been any one of us, who through negligence, bad investments, embezzlement, theft or dishonesty misappropriated the king's resources.

Of course, the servant didn't have the money, so the king commanded that he and his family be sold to reconcile the debt and punish the dishonest servant. The servant begged, pleaded for his and the freedom of his family. His brokenness, humble spirit and repentance moved the king's heart to compassion and pity. The king wouldn't satisfy his right to justice or revenge on such a foolish and irresponsible man.

Therefore, to satisfy his own heart, the king forgave the debt, accepted the wrong, but permanently dismissed the servant from his position. He thought that by handling the matter this way, the servant, being free from prison, could get employment someplace else; plus the king thought that by being merciful, he would gain at great expense a forever grateful friend.

However the servant conveniently forgot what had just happened to him. Though he was elated at being loosed from that million-dollar headache that almost got him and his family sold on the auction block. He found a fellow servant who owed him a few measly dollars. Immediately, his old, greedy unforgiving nature returned with vengeance; he was still angry because he'd gotten caught stealing the king's loot.

He had been humiliated and wanted to take it out on another person; he was embarrassed, shamed at losing his job, and everyone in the kingdom knew of it. He grabbed the fellow servant by the throat, choked him, and raved, "Give me my money!" His fellow servant, not a violent man, humbly pleaded, "Give me some more time." But he would not; he threw him in prison. The neighbors saw what happened. The king's servant was abusive, unforgiving and arrogant. He didn't do his dirty deed in a corner, but wanted others to see how ruthless, how controlling and dominating he was. He also wanted his fellow servant to suffer his failures---how he was proud but made pitiful before the king; the king had him on his knees begging like a whimpering pup; he wanted his fellow servant to plead for his freedom too.

Then the servant would get personal satisfaction by saying "No!" The king was wroth: "You wicked servant! I forgave you all that debt---shouldn't you have forgiven your fellow servant that debt?" He delivered him to the tormentors. The parable concludes: "So likewise shall My heavenly Father do also unto you, if you from your hearts forgive not his brother their trespasses" (Matthew 18:23-35). Like the servant in the parable was accountable to the king, so are Christians accountable to Jehovah-Elohim, to handle His accounts.

The earthly king forgave but didn't restore the dishonest servant back to his position; it's equally true that when someone trespasses against us, we must forgive, but restoring the trespasser to his former position---friend, lover, wife, husband, priest, pastor, teacher, lawyer, businessperson---is optional, a matter of the trespasser becoming trustworthy again, plus a willingness on our part to accept him back with confidence that he won't betray us again.

Sometimes these trust issues take time to work out; sometimes they cannot be worked out. As children of God, we have Elohim-Life inside our spirit to help us overcome demonic traits such as a spirit of Unforgiveness. We were all wicked servants, robbing God every chance we got; we were devote sinners on our way to a fiery Hell; we were lost, having only one hope to survive the schemes of the Devil; that Blessed Hope was Jesus Christ. We owed a debt that we could not pay; He paid a debt that He did not owe.

Like the king in the parable, God had every right to turn us over to the tormentors, the hounds of Hell. Instead He forgave us of our sin debt. It's true that Jesus Christ died on the cross for all sinners, that is, those who believe in Him, but not so we can continue to sin, or have legal or spiritual rights to our particular sin. Jesus didn't die upon the cross for us to use His death as an excuse to continue in sin, since He already died once for sin. Neither can we use the worn out phrases: "I'm only human, I'm not perfect, or, God's not done with me yet" excuses, though all of these statements are true, but not valid reasons to continue in sin. The servant misused Forgiveness; he thought that it gave him freedom and a license to continue in his old thieving and manipulative ways. We must never fall this trap. Through God's Salvation Plan in which Forgiveness of sins was paramount. God accepted our apology and faith. He granted us the free gift of Salvation.

Jesus Christ took our sin debt and exchanged it for His righteousness. He justified us by declaring the sin indictment against us no longer valid. Jesus struck the gabble and legally pronounced us Not Guilty due to His Mercy triumphing over Judgment, the balancing of our sin account drawn against His inexhaustible righteousness account in Christ Jesus. The king's servant desperately wanted and needed a way out of his incredible debt.

He was aware that physical punishment was an option; another option he and his family being sold; still, he and his family could have been executed or imprisoned for life. But the king's decree of Forgiveness wiped the servant's slate clean; Forgiveness and debt cancellation was an out-of-this-world heavenly decision!

When a Christian fails to walk in the Spirit of the Word others see it too. The mean things we say and do to others---the threats of violence and actual contact---are similar to the servant's behavior with his fellow servant. We must be "delivered" from our old self-life, our past negative, old man emotions, feeling and dramatic experiences; our past will fight to make an appearance in the present, try to live again; the feelings and secret prejudices of our worldly past must be taken to the cross to suffer death, then the emotional function of self will be resurrected to an adequate, secure and righteous way of felling and having compassion for others.

Angels, spirits and human beings are watching. The wicked servant was delivered to the tormentors. These men weren't only prison guards but depraved sadist; they tortured the prisoners. Symbolically, this part of the parable describes the remanding into custody of the unforgiving person to Satan. Then Satan's demons will torment (like King Saul) us while we are on earth--until we decide to heed the Word of God. But if we resist the Word and die, the evil demons in Hell take custody and possession of us, a permanent Certificate of Incarceration, to bind and torture us. God will deal with us the way we deal with others: "...as you have done it unto the least of these My brethren, you have done it unto Me" (Mt. 25:40).

What Manner Of Woman This Is!

"And behold, a woman in the city, which was a sinner, when she knew that Jesus sat at meat in the Pharisee's house, brought an alabaster box of ointment. 41"There was a certain creditor, which had two debtors: The one owed five hundred pence, and the other fifty. 42 And when they had nothing to pay, he frankly forgave them both"---Lk. 7.37,41-43.

Simon, a Pharisee invited Jesus to his home for a meal. Simon was a member of the Sanhedrin Council, the seventy-member Jewish Supreme Court consisting of Pharisees and Sadducees. We don't know if Simon was a relative of Jesus, His disciples, friend or was only curious of Jesus' ministry. But before long, a woman burst into the room; she was uninvited, didn't even knock or introduce herself—and stood at Jesus' feet as He reclined at the table.

She broke open an alabaster box of sweet-smelling ointment; it wasn't unusual of people to give Jesus and His disciples meals and money offerings; many people adored and were supportive of Him—yet, this woman was on a mission: Like the three wise men who came to the baby Jesus as He laid in a manger, this woman was on a worshipping mission. She stood at His feet and wept.

She washed His feet with her hot tears and wiped His feet with her hair. She lovingly kissed His feet and anointed them with ointment. She humbled herself before the cloud of witnesses in Heaven and earth. Her eyes were on Jesus.

Simon was disgusted. His heart rebelled, and he may have thought: "Look what the cat has dragged in. How did this whore get into my house? That dumb servant of mine must have fallen asleep! The nerve of this harlot defiling my guest!" Jesus actually read Simon's "mail": "This Man, if He were a Prophet, would have known what manner of woman this is that touches Him: for she is a sinner." Jesus knew Simon's thoughts; Jesus knew the hearts of everyone who came around Him; In general, He knew the thoughts and intent of the hearts of all men—that the hearts of men were deceitful and desperately wicked. He wouldn't allow Himself to be used by man. Jesus used the Parable of the Creditor and the Debtor.

He wasn't giving a discourse on management, accounting or banking, but a lesson on the spiritual value of Forgiveness blossoming forth through Spiritual Love. All Jesus' messages were designed to get to the source of man's bondage to the world: The lack of Agape Love in the human spirit of man was why Forgiveness from the heart was missing. Under the Mosaic Law, this woman was a sinner; but under the same Law all mankind were sinners---so what made her sin any different than this Pharisee?

Could Simon morally cast the first stone? This woman didn't bring her expensive and precious ointment to impress Jesus or Simon the Pharisee, nor was her motive to buy Forgiveness, but to emotionally demonstrate the fruit of her repentance. She brought forth, as John the Baptist declared, fruit showing forth the works of Repentance. She was godly sorry for her sinful lifestyle; godly sorrow leads to Repentance. Her sins had caused her and her family great ridicule and suffering. It grieved her to live the immoral profession she had chosen perhaps out of poverty.

She sought Forgiveness in the manner that was natural to her personality. In the eyes of the Lord Jesus---where it mattered--- she had faithfully worshipped Him like no legion of Cherubim could. Her faith was accounted to her as righteousness. She was forgiven.

Simon didn't see her fruit. He sat in the position to judge according to the interpretation of the Letter of the Law. He didn't possess the ability to be a compassionate judge, but an interpreter of facts and figures. Simon didn't see with his spirit eyes through her sin to see the person who committed the sin; he couldn't see a soul in dire need of being released from the Devil. Her soul cried out for Forgiveness, but the cry fell on Simon's deaf, religious ears.

Because of his legalistic unforgiving heart, Simon didn't believe that she deserved or was entitled to another chance at life. In truth, Simon was bound by a different chain, an Unforgiveness chain; he was tightly bound. He wasn't free and neither would she be if Simon had anything to do with it; Once a whore always a whore was Simon's opinion (and many today think the same). Jesus had one more lesson to teach. It was customary for the host to furnish his visiting traveler with a kiss, then a servant provided water to wash the traveler's feet, and anointing oil for freshening up.

"And He turned to the woman, and said unto Simon, See thou this woman? I entered into your house, you gave Me no water for My feet; but she hath washed My feet with her tears, and wiped them with the hairs of her head.

You gave Me no kiss; but this woman since the time I came in has not ceased to kiss My feet. My head with oil you did not anoint; but this woman has anointed My feet with ointment...Her sins, which are many, are forgiven; for she loves much; but to whom little is forgiven, the same loves little." (Lk.7:44-47).

When Victims Won't Forgive

It's likely that we have sought Forgiveness through our family, friends, those we have offended or victimized while pursuing our profession or lifestyle. We have asked for Forgiveness but received rejection, anger or silence instead; or maybe we don't know how to approach God with our request, or don't know whether it's appropriate to forgive ourselves for our own peace and sanity when others won't.

When we have hurt someone and sincerely ask for Forgiveness and they won't grant it (they think that by not granting Forgiveness that we are forever un-forgiven or cursed), we can then go to God to obtain Forgiveness; and though that person may never forgive us, the fact that we have asked them releases us from them (but they remain bound in Unforgiveness) but as children of God can always go to God about the matter. After we have received God's Forgiveness---and we will know in our spirit that we have received Forgiveness because of the peace in the heart and the sense of the burden lifted off of us—then we have permission to forgive ourselves. Forgiving ourselves can be a complex matter; we may have to say it many times, then live as though we are forgiven, by doing those thing that forgiven people do.

But remember, we cannot forgive ourselves until we have asked the offended (if possible and practical) and God. Otherwise, criminals— murders and rapist would commit crimes, forgive themselves that same hour, and with a clear conscious, commit more crimes; and there are some who commit heinous crimes while having no conscious, remorse, and will not repent or stop until incarcerated or death overtakes them! Every person who earnestly desires Forgiveness for his or her sins can receive it from God through the Lord Jesus Christ; God knows that He gave us the ability to remember our past but no ability to change it. Forgiveness is the only way to make peace with our past and leave it in the past; so we take our burdens to the Lord and leave them there.

CHAPTER SIX

Agape Love

"For God so loved (agape) the world, that He gave His only begotten Son, that whosoever believes in Him should not perish, but have everlasting life" John 3.16.

It's wonderful to be alive and a new creature in Christ Jesus. The old things are passing away; behold, all things are become new. The life we now live, the **Agape Love** of Christ within us compels us to go on to higher heights in serving Him. Through the greatness of Jesus Christ, God reconciled, united us to Himself. God is Agape Love (1 Jn. 4:8). He chose Love as the avenue to reach and gravitate us to Himself.

Love is more than an attribute of God but actually the Life of His Being. His living, vibrant Love moving, expressing Himself to ever greater measures in our spirit is evidence and a reminder that we're becoming more like His Son than when we were lost in the world. Even the unsaved can tell we're Christians by our Love. Love covers a multitude of sins. The Holy Bible describes four types of Love. First, in the Greek Language, there's **Eros Love**: This type of love is sexual love; it involves the entire interaction of a person's sensual, mental, volitional, emotional and physical participation; this love often results in sexual intercourse between a man and a woman.

This type of love is human, natural, instinctive; the sexual intercourse function is only acceptable to God through holy matrimony called marriage. Other sexual relationships other than male-to-female unions are strictly forbidden. Eros Love is conditional, subject to change by either participant, with time, situation or circumstance. Next is **Phileo Love:** This type of love consist of unity, closeness, friendship such as with, friends and coworkers. This type of love is nonsexual; but a friend of the opposite sex can become a lover. Eros and Phileo Love are present in the unsaved and saved individuals, because both loves are a product of the mind/soul body. This type of love is conditional, subject to change with time, situation or circumstance. Third is **Storge Love:** This type of is refers to familial love. It is evident, for example, in the warm affection that parents have toward their children. Next is **Agape Love**: Spiritual Love. Agape Love is the highest expression of Love; it's Jehovah-Elohim Himself. Agape Love is the first Fruit of the Spirit, and the character of God; it's the manifestation and expression of the invisible God. Agape Love doesn't originate in or through sexual attraction, emotions, feelings, intelligence, imaginations, external senses, or depend on situation, circumstance or friendship.

Agape Love is unconditional Love; God's Love is impersonal; He's no respecter of persons---He loves sinners and saints with equal measure. His Love-Life seeks an object to indwell and reflect, like a mirror, off of; this Love-Life seeks its (His) level, the greatest heights, width and depths, in whomever comes into contact with Him. Agape Love is the basic involuntary response of the immutable Jehovah-Elohim. One must be Born Again to possess Agape Love.

The force behind the Life of Jehovah-Elohim is Agape Love. The other two types of love come from the human consciousness. In the human psychology, relationships and experience, the lower loves have their purpose, but Agape Love operates in our spirit-consciousness bearing witness to God's Love for us, and that we're children of God. Not only do we perceive His character rising in us, but can live His character in the world. Most people think of love as an emotion or the sexual aspect of it; but God isn't emotional---and the only begotten Son He has was created without intercourse or emotion!

God isn't subject to responses, reactions or conclusions based on feelings or emotions. Everything He does is in accordance with His intrinsic nature: Love, Word, Holiness, Righteousness, Justice, Grace, Mercy and Forgiveness. Even His righteous indignation, His "kindled" anger are intrinsic to His nature. Through the path of Love, we can probe into God's innermost Self and explore to discover who He is, and why so many saints before us made Him their life. Our Salvation is centered upon God's Love for us; it has nothing to do with our love for God.

After we realized and perceived in our spirit the Agape love of God towards us, then we sought to love Him back. Agape Love is the only

Love that God possesses; but as a human being Jesus of Nazareth possessed Agape, Phileo, and Eros love--this isn't to imply that Jesus had sexual intercourse, but to state that He was human in every way; He had a mother, relatives and friends He loved; He laughed or wept because He had human feelings. God isn't a respecter of persons; He loves us as much as He loves His Jesus. This is evident in that before the foundation of the world, the great Love of Jehovah-Elohim compelled Him to consult the counsel of His will--the Elohim commonalty---to expedite a plan of Salvation. Christ, the Word was chosen, foreordained to incarnate in the earth and become the only begotten Son of God.

As the Son of God, Christ became the prearranged way that God would accept mankind back into Heaven. God so loved His creation called Man, that He sent His Word into the world to become His Son, to recover the Man that was lost in sin, who lost his dominion, and restore Him to his rightful position as a son; that if the Man who is lost in the world would believe, trust in, cleave to, rely on the Son of God, he would be conformed to His image and likeness, become a joint-heir with Jesus Christ.

4 "Hear, 0 Israel: The LORD our God is one LORD:

5 And thou shall love the LORD thy God with all your heart, and with all thy soul, and with all thy might" Deu. 6.4,5.

"Thou shall not avenge, nor bear any grudge against the children of thy people, but thou shall **love thy neighbor as thyself**: I AM the LORD"---Lev. 19.18. 36.

36 "Master, which is the Great Commandment in the Law?

37 Jesus said unto him, You shall love the Lord your God with all your heart, and with all your soul, and with all your mind.

38 This is the first and Great Commandment.

39 And the second is like unto it, You shall love your neighbor as yourself.

40 On these two Commandments hang all the Law and the prophets"

A lawyer of the Mosaic Law was present to test Jesus. The religious Jews had classified over six hundred laws and often debated over which ones were more important. The lawyer, hoping to lure Jesus into a debate, hoping to trap Him or expose to the people a weakness in His doctrine, challenged Jesus. Since the question was one of importance, Jesus answered for the benefit of the people, and not necessary for the lawyer, who, already knew the answer to his own question. Jesus knew the scriptures better than anyone; as the Christ He was the One who gave the Law to the Jews.

Jesus skillfully quoted from the scriptures the two Books of Moses: Deuteronomy and Leviticus. He explained that both of these Commandments were given by the one God; that by fulfilling the two Commandments and making them a part of their daily lives, they would fulfill the moral requirements of the Books of the Law and the Books of the Prophets.

Jesus taught His audience to focus on the Spirit of the Law, the spiritual meaning behind the Letter of the Law. God never told the Jews to love Him with their spirit; neither did Jesus tell the Jews to love God with their spirit. The reason for this is that man wasn't capable of loving God with his spirit, because man was spiritually dead---devoid of habitation of the Spirit of God, who is Agape Love; but God and Jesus commanded the people to Phileo Love God with all the heart, the soul, with its functions of the intellect, emotions, imagination and will; then, Phileo Love their neighbor as themselves.

Love for God and the neighbor was more important than whole burnt offerings. In these New Testament times, the Dispensation of Grace, we have the Spirit of God indwelling us; we have greater capacity to love because of the Agape Love present in our human spirit. The path of Agape Love---unconditional love---fulfills the requirements of Christ-like Christian character.

The Agape Love manifested in our spirit should compel us, like Jesus, to stretch forth our hands and heal the sick, loose the oppressed, and witness to the lost in Jesus' Name. This Love was given to us to give to others; the Love of God was given to us without measure, was manifested in our heart by the Holy Ghost which has been given unto us. In demonstrating the greatness of the Name of Jesus Christ and for sake of Love, God reconciled the world of fallen men unto Himself, and didn't count our trespasses against us, but sent His Son to die on the cross as a Prince and Savior. Yet, the lawyer couldn't have known what we know about the greatness of Jesus Christ. The lawyer and the religious Jews rewrote the scriptures; their interpretations and teachings left out what God said not to, "avenge" or "grudge," but "Thou shall love thy neighbor as thyself." The legalistic Jews wanted to punish anyone who broke the slightest rule, ordinance, tradition or law. The Jews believed that they were justified in punishing transgressors because they were only guardians of the Mosaic Law. "An eye for an eye and a tooth for a tooth"---they demanded to receive legal retribution. There was no room for love---except for their own family and friends; love your friends and hate your enemies, was what they taught the people.

The Mosaic Law was given to Israel because of their lack of faith and obedience to the Word of God. Israel wanted to will and do what was right in their own eyes; they desired to hate rather than love one another. Sin had infiltrated and reigned in their hearts to such an extent, the practice of Phileo Love as prescribed by the Commandments to cure what ailed their souls was ignored; the absence of faith, obedience and love, moved Jehovah-Elohim to institute the Mosaic Law to teach the Jews about the necessity of love. As the Law exposed sin and made Israel conscious of their thoughts and behaviors, now the Messiah walked among them to put the finishing touch, to teach about love, the fulfillment of the Law.

The Mosaic Law was a tutor, a teacher of faith; the Law taught obedience to God's Word; in the daily practice of the scriptures, faith developed a leaning of the entire being and personality on God's Word, and "faith works by love" (Ga. 5:6).

To walk in **Faith** is also walking in **Love**! God's unconditional Love becomes strongest in us when we give His Love away; the more Love we radiate from us the more Love will gravitate to us. The purpose of Love is to woo the lost! Glorious Love surges like a mighty river. Love seeks its level and overflows the banks of our heart. That Christian in whom the Love of God flows in and out of stands in the eternity between Heaven and earth, being in this world yet not of it. Love breaks the traditions of men and brings revival. Love is like an exploding super nova, or water racing over the edge of a thunderous beautiful, wonderful, dynamic, breathtaking, refreshing, restoring our spiritually dry bones.

1 "If I speak in the tongues of men and angels, but have not love, I am only a sounding gong or a clanging cymbal. 2 If I have the gift of prophecy and can fathom all mysteries and all knowledge...but have not love, I am nothing"---1 Cor. 13.1,2.

The Apostle Paul wrote to the Corinthians about the importance of Love. The Corinthian Church was bustling with Spiritual Gifts, the manifestations of the power of Jehovah-Elohim, but was lacking in Christ-like character, honesty, truth and integrity. Their moral behavior was selfish, prideful, lusty and immoral---equal to the unbelievers.

Paul counseled them from the abundance of revelations that he received personally from the Lord Jesus Christ. He told them that though they had these spiritual manifestations of the Holy Spirit in their congregation, wasn't proof positive that they were mature Christians, or that Jesus Christ had placed His seal of approval on their lives. He wrote that God's Love for the world of lost sinners and His own saints was the primary reason why He entrusted the gifts to them, that these gifts were useful for the advancement of the Kingdom of God, and not for personal vain glory.

Paul stated that the Spiritual Gift of Speaking in Tongues or the other eight gifts, without being motivated by Love in the heart of the practitioner, was like the unwanted noise of clanging cymbals, a distraction from the real purpose of the gift---Love. Paul wasn't against the use of Spiritual Gifts, but the abuse of the gifts in the church assembly. He stated that all the Spiritual Gifts work harmoniously---Jesus as the Conductor and we the Christians as the musicians with instruments--to play a beautiful Love song.

The gifts excel according to the measure of Love allowed to flow out of the Believer; the incoming measure is the same with all Believers, but the outgoing measure is subject to the will, faith, attitude and spiritual maturity of the Believer; the more free-flowing, unobstructed Love, the more tangible the manifestations of the Spirit in our ministry will be; less Love brings less fruit, less people converted for the Lord of the Harvest. Again, "faith works by Love" (Gal. 5:6). Faith that works by Love should be the motto of the church today. Without Love we're just a private club, meeting on Sunday morning and pretending to be something that we're not, and basically making a lot of noise! Unless the Love of Jesus is present, unless we labor in His Name, it's all smoke and mirrors, an illusionist's performance in front of a packed audience. Love is longsuffering and is characterized by humility. Love loves the truth. Love enables us to weather the hardships of life. Love cannot fail or lose its power. Love is Elohim-Life. Since God has reigned gloriously throughout eternity, His Love has not lessened. His Love has sounded the depths throughout Heaven and earth like a continuous symphony; music that holds the listener's heart poised on eagle's wings high above the world.

Through Love we were apprehended by God; then we became hearers and doers of the Word of God. Now we Love and appreciate the truth. New converts are apprehended, drawn by the Father to the Son for Salvation; they're drawn by the love of Love, His Word of Love towards them. New Believers also experience the deep, deep Love of Jesus from contact with His messengers. It's Love that gravitates sinners to Christ; other works can't take the place of genuine Love in our heart towards the lost and hurting. No matter what we do in ministering to the saved or unsaved it must originate by and through heart-inspired Love. Agape Love is real, a tangible reality.

We either have the genuine article or a forgery. If our Love isn't real, it's only a matter of time before the farce is exposed. People can "feel" in their heart whether we truly Love them or are motivated by a sense of religious duty in our acceptance of them. And when personal trials and tribulations come to test our Love, the melting heat of a blast furnace, only Agape Love can past the test!

Because time is running out, and this world scene will be rolled up like an ancient scroll, we don't have time to be playing children's games of dress-up, and playing church. Instead of pounding on the Gates of Heaven asking for Spiritual Gifts, let's consider allowing a greater measure of Agape Love to flow through us, out of our heart and into the world. Agape Love is a different manifestation of God's spiritual power.

The Person of Jehovah-Elohim, Jesus Christ resides in **Faith**, **Hope** and **Love**--but the greatest of these is Love (1 Cor. 13:13).

22 "But the Fruit of the Spirit is Love, Joy, Peace, Patience, Kindness, Good-

ness, Faithfulness, 23 Gentleness and Self-Control..." Gal. 5.22, 23.

The Fruit of the Spirit, the character traits of God, like the Vine and the Branch, become the Fruit of the resurrected, Born Again human spirit. Without Agape Love we can't do anything of an eternal nature. The Phileo and Eros Love feelings and emotions we have towards others are but shadows and types of the divine essence; our human love is but momentary spurts of an internal geyser full of fuzzy feelings, sensitivity, friendship, sensual and sexual passions of marriage unity---compared to the Presence of God in the spirit, perception and realization of eternal acceptance and security, the confidence that we're children of God whose destiny is to reign with Him in perfect Love.

The Fruit of Agape Love is the first mentioned of the nine. Love is the *starter fruit* which, like a blasting cap, sets the other Fruit off. Love, because it's God-Life, is the former and latter rain of the Holy Spirit, causes the other Fruit to grow and mature. In cooperation with the Holy Spirit, we must allow the Fruit of Love to exert itself (Himself).

The integrity of Love, the Name of Jesus, goes with us wherever we go. Love is our constant companion; but Spiritual Gifts only manifest as needed and we cannot will them to manifest. Yet we can will that Love will by faith flow from our spirit, that Love will greet every-one we meet on our spiritual journey through time and space.

Love: The Missing Link

Jesus explained to the Jews in His audience the importance of Phileo Love, and how the previous teachers had missed the mark in interpreting the provisions for love in the Mosaic Law. The Earth-bound Church also needs to consider the worth of Agape Love, the missing link. The world is a love-starved place. We, as an Unsaved person, are searching for Agape Love and looking in the wrong places.

Our soul is searching for its soul mate—its counterpart, the human spirit, who is dead, unresponsive to our soul, but can be resurrected by the Holy Spirit. Because our spirit is dead without Christ, our soul cannot fellowship or perceive it with its mental functions and senses. Therefore, we think our soul mate is another soul, a human being: The truth is we're unconsciously searching for Jesus.

Our soul's desire is to be filled with Christ, the Love of Life. Are we searching for unconditional Love in all the wrong places? We have trudged this raging planet in search of the one whose soul we long for. Not knowing that our search isn't for a human mate, we looked and continue to look for Agape Love---for Jesus Christ in several human relationships. We crave and require intimacy, having someone close to confide in and experience life with. When trials and tribulations, boredom and dissatisfaction comes, we fall out of Phileo Love with people.

Perhaps, our marriage involving Eros Love has failed, but we believe that we are healed from that relationship, and are searching for a new partner, hoping, with an eye out for that Boaz or Abigail elusive soul mate. We are searching for Agape Love, thinking that it originates in the sensual realm, the realm of the flesh. Years have passed; it has been a monumental waste of time! Jesus Christ is our Soul Mate: But in search of love, we have even had children. These children, whom we dearly love, arrived in and out of wedlock, but are now unhappy and insecure because we are again out searching for love, and are not around very much.

And this causes the children's family, school and social lives to be unstable. Even the children being born becomes a disadvantage while searching for a soul mate. Yet, the children, searching for meaning to life and acceptance, pick up our unhappiness, the misplaced anger, resentment, dysfunction and bitterness at feeling short-changed in love.

Love Is Healing

"Peter answered and said unto Him, Though all men shall be offended because of You, yet never will I be offended. Jesus said...before the cock crow, you shall deny Me three times"---Mt. 26.33.

Peter loved Jesus. He loved Jesus with all the love he had. Peter was confident that neither Hell or high water could separate him from the Master; and being offended because of Him was nonsense. Earlier in the ministry Peter demonstrated his devotion when many of the disgruntled disciples stopped following Jesus. When Jesus asked the remaining twelve, Peter said, "To whom shall we go, You have the words of Eternal Life."

Throughout the ministry years, Peter had been harassed and ridiculed by the members of the Sanhedrin Council, Herodians, Zealots and other religious groups, because the teachings of Jesus were controversial. Jesus drew enormous crowds, and equally enormous persecution and hostility, which was also directed towards His disciples. Yet Peter loved Jesus and accepted the challenge. Jesus' words to Peter were, "Come ye after Me" (Mk. 1:17). Jesus didn't choose Peter because he was perfect; Peter was quite impulsive. Jesus gave him a new name: The stone. Jesus chose Peter for what he would be not what he was; Jehovah-Elohim included Peter in His plan as an Apostle of the Lamb.

In choosing disciples, Jesus looked for souls who wanted to change, those who wanted their lives to count for a divine purpose. Jesus ordained souls to be converted by His Love. He chose disciples who were available, teach-able and usable to communicate His teachings and produce divine fruit. Peter made a lot of mistakes; but God knew Peter before He actually called him to follow Jesus. Peter was a fisherman with very limited formal education; he spoke without thinking.

One day Jesus asked Peter, "Who do men say that I am?" Peter responded with his heart confession, "You are the Christ, the Son of the living God." Joy flood *Jesus.* He replied, "Flesh and blood did not reveal that to you, but the Father" (Mt.16:16,17).

Then Satan struck Peter down: 73 "...Surely you are one of them

[Jesus' disciples, for your accent gives you away. 74 Then he began calling down curses on himself and he swore to them, "I don't know the Man!" Immediately the rooster crowed. 75 ...And he went outside and wept bitterly" ---Mt. 26.73-75.

When the words of denial fell from Peter's lips, it was shocking news to him. He remembered what Jesus had told him earlier, that before the rooster crowed he would deny Him three times. Though Peter's tongue strained not to deny his love--Phileo devotion to Jesus--the spirit of fear seized him and wouldn't let him go until he denied knowing the Prince of Life.

Peter discovered in that moment of desperation that there was something wrong, deficient, depleted or unformed in his heart; that something was Agape Love---Christ formed in his spirit. Peter cursed the day he was born; he was ashamed and regretted his very life on earth; he came down hard on himself for being so weak, fearful and unbelieving; he coward down to a noisy servant girl. Peter had natural, self-life confidence; but Agape Love, not Phileo Love had to be the backbone to the bold words he previously confessed: "I will not be offended!" Peter went away dumbstruck, his heart torn by his lying lips. He was broken, and would've given anything to take back his words.

Peter needed to be healed. After Jesus resurrected from the dead, the angel told the women at the sepulcher, "...tell His disciples and Peter that He goes before you into Galilee" (Mk. 16:7). Jesus knew that Peter was hurting---and bad. The Savior sent word to him that he was Loved, accepted and cherished as one of His disciples.

15 "So when they had dined, Jesus said to Simon Peter, Simon, son of Jonas, do you love (Agape) Me more than these? He said to Him, Yea Lord; You know I love (phileo) You. He said to him, Feed My lambs.

16 He said to him again the second time, Simon, son of Jonas, do you love (agape) Me? He said to him, Yea Lord; You know that I love (phileo) You. He said to him, Feed My sheep.

17 He said to him the third time, Simon, son of Jonas, do you love (phileo) Me? And he said to Him, Lord, You know all things; You know that I love (phileo) You..." John 21.15-17.

After Jesus' resurrection, He showed Himself three times to the disciples. On this occasion Peter, James and John went back to their occupation as fishermen; though Jesus had called them to be fishers of men, the love of the sea was still in them. They sat around the fire and ate fish and bread. After dining, Jesus asked Peter a question: Do you Love Me more than these fishes? At first it appeared that Jesus was joking with Peter, but He wasn't. Jesus lead Peter to the darkness and inadequacy inside his self-life that led to the present trauma.

Jesus got to the root of his denial. Then Jesus led him through the anguish of his bitter heart at turning his back on the Son of God; his denial wasn't as devastating and irredeemable as when Judas Iscariot betrayed Jesus, went out and hung himself---but Peter denied the Lord and cursed himself with his own mouth, curses that had to be undone. Three times Peter cursed and denied Jesus; three times Jesus questioned Peter's loyalty: Peter revealed the abundance of his heart, where his treasure was stored, and Jesus was satisfied. Jesus wanted a faithful Peter, a man with a servant's heart: Feed My lambs---My new Converts, and, Feed My Sheep, the Body of Christ. Peter had repented--that wasn't the issue. Jesus knew why Peter denied Him and wanted Peter to know too. Jesus asked him twice, Do you Love (Agape) Me? But Peter keep replying, You know that I love (phileo) You.

That was the issue---Peter's inner strength arose from his friendship with the Son of God: Satan manipulated that friendship and Peter momentarily regarded his relationship with Jesus as friendship, an arrangement when convenient, but expendable when inconvenient. Peter had mental devotion and emotional love for Jesus, but no unconditional Agape Love. Peter didn't understand what the Love of God was.

He thought that Love emanated from Jesus because He is the Christ, the Son of God. Even now Peter experienced the Love of Jesus as He smiled compassionately at him; that warm smile was healing his soul. Peter didn't know that he too could be filled with the Master's Love. The third time Jesus lowered the bar. He substituted Agape for Phileo and asked a question, Are you at least My friend? Peter knew that there was a valuable lesson for him to learn about Love.

Love Sets Us Free

In the same way that it is for freedom that Christ has set us free, it is for Love that he has also set us free. The lack of genuine Love in the world and even in the churches has caused may to become religious and easily provoked to anger; it has also causes many to be suspicious and unwilling to socialize within the church, that is, not extending our friendship and fellowship to get to know the person in the seat beside us; we sing songs, worship, even pray at the altar with literal strangers because the Fruit of Love is not flowing in the congregation as the Spiritual Gifts are. Spiritual character, the Love of Christ and His integrity is lacking in the local churches.

We must continuous pray for the Fruit of the Spirit, and not be more persistent on receiving and developing Spiritual Gifts, titles and positions, without the character to uphold the office, dignity and honor of God.

Passing From Death To Life

"He that Loves his brother abides in the Light, and there is no occasion of stumbling in him. But he that hates his brother is in darkness, and knows not where he goes, because the darkness has blinded his eyes"—1 Jn. 2.10. John the Beloved Disciple was satisfied with the Person of Jesus Christ. He was satisfied with the centrality of Christ and the divine revelations concerning Him.

John's goal in life was to lead others to the rest he discovered in Jesus Christ, a rest so desperately needed for the weak and huddled masses yearning to be free. John stated that he had seen, heard and handled the Word of Life. He found no darkness or negativity in God; so we as Christians must be careful to see, touch, and handle Life and not death. John believed and wrote that if we walk in the Light of God's Love, that the Blood of Jesus Christ cleanses us from all sins; that sin cannot come to the Light---Love would dry up sin at its root. The Lord commanded that we Love one another as He loves us, and gave Himself for us, as a sweet-smelling Savior; this means esteeming others ahead of ourselves. Love is sacrificial and purpose-driven. Loving our brother, than is, someone other than ourselves is walking in the Light of the revelation of Christ. He said, "Do this in remembrance of Me;" this Commandment doesn't only apply to Communion but to Love also. If we would Love as Jesus loves, the Blessing will come upon and overtake us. Strangers would go out their way to bless us.

We may never know the specifics of why they are being so generous and kind to us: But God commanded them to bless us. The enemy of Love is hate because the enemy of Jehovah-Elohim is Satan. God reigns gloriously by the Light of His Love. The rulers of the darkness of this world strive to quench God's Love attraction by deceiving us, blinding our mind with hate and revenge; he knows we need Christ as our Life---our true soul mate. Those who are looking for a soul mate in the natural realm are being deceived, lured into a lifelong fleshly pursuit.

The darkness that John wrote about, the hatred, violence, racism and anti-Christian doctrines are invisible shackles to bind us; they keep us from the Excellency of the knowledge of Christ Jesus, and in blind pursuit of human the human loves. Now that we are aware of the Love of God, His plans, purposes and pursuits, we cannot afford to be complacent or passive with a "do my own thing" or "have it my way" philosophy. This type of thinking isn't new---it's a Genesis favorite lifestyle; it's the very lifestyle that directed the anger of the Lord against the Hebrews Nation. Any religion or philosophy that isn't based on God's Love for the individual and man-kind is worthless. These liberal--it's all good--beliefs are an assorted mixture of self-exaltation, religious error, mysticism and psychology; it is repackaged rebellion, warmed-over and served by Satan's propaganda editorial staff.

His staff has the latest mental manipulation techniques, escapisms, pleasures and Time-Wasters. Love-less religions separate mankind from the greatest of all lovers—God! The century-old repackaged religions are sweetened with some truth, given to appointed human vessels to proclaim and even die for as being Heaven-sent; these satanic verses appeal to the souls that have a desire to go to Heaven but don't want to change—slay the self-life. Religions without Agape

Love are self-made "paths" to Heaven; they supply an abundance of zeal, emotion and false security; they are only a Nichol-plated chain---compared to a plain steel chain---to bind and preoccupy us with empty but attractive rituals of legalism, until we are worn out and a candidate for the bone yard. Religion without Agape Love invites spirits of murder, sickness, disease, poverty, violence, murder, infidelity, hatred and suicide into our lives: these spirits come because we are embracing false doctrine.

An example of this is Cain and Abel. Abel exercised his Faith in God and was declared righteous. The outward expression of his Faith in Jehovah-Elohim, was that He accepted his love sacrifice; this sacrifice included the blood of the lamb---a typology of Jesus slain on the cross of Calvary. Cain's religion was based upon his own selfish desires. He reasoned that the end justified the means.

He believed, like many people today, that God would accept whatever offered to Him. Cain reasoned that obedience and loving God was secondary to sacrifice, that he was doing God a favor by even acknowledging Him. Filled with foolish pride, Cain didn't take God seriously; he didn't believe that he was a sinner or that Satan had hardened his heart towards God, Adam, Eve, and Abel.

Satan persuaded him to stand up for his right to live his own life the way he pleased, to do what was right in his own eyes. Cain lived a sin-conscious lifestyle; his consciousness accused him, taunted him daily with evil imaginations, denial, shame, blame, jealousy and bitterness; he was self-deceived about the noble purposes of God, and his place in the world. Secretly, the Phileo Love Cain had departed from him: Satan stole it. God rejected Cain's works, his first fruits; God refused to accept and honor Cain's faithless attitude, bloodless sacrifice, and loveless religion.

Abel produced works consisted with his love and obedience to God. He possessed a righteousness-consciousness free of accusations. His life was one of repentance, for he dared not claim innocence, but confessed that he was a sinner; he trusted in and relied on the Love of God. But Cain had a wicked and hateful heart. Cain's offering was cursed along with his way of thinking---because his material offering came from the cursed ground, and his religious thoughts from cursed Satan.

The love that once brought joy, peace and goodness in Cain's life, was replaced by evil imaginations towards his brother: then Cain murdered Abel. John reminded us of the story of Cain and Abel because John had spent' his entire adult life preaching a Gospel based upon the Love of Jesus Christ. Many of the religions of his day were based upon law, tradition, or a unity that amounted to Phileo.

Today, there are all types of so-called paths to Heaven, enlightenment, peace, tranquility, spirit guides, or to heal the "inner child. Because these paths are predominately Phileo---humanity based---they often become as perverted as the Baal high places in the Old Testament, where sexual promiscuity, orgies, homosexuality, abuse, child molestations, animal and human sacrifices are not uncommon practices in some religions and cults; fanatics, serial killers and terrorists are often bread from these types of religions. Therefore, John wrote, "Whosoever hates his brother is a murderer; and you know that no murderer (who hasn't repented and accepted Jesus Christ) has eternal life abiding in him" (1 Jn. 3:15).

Passing from death to Eternal Life involves Love; without this Love, we are no better than a unrepentant murderer. Murdering someone is not always physical--it can be assassinating character, lying, slander, gossip, rejecting, exclusion, hating, misusing or just plain refusing to pay the debt of loving others.

In basic social relationships, with Phileo and Eros Loves, both being conditional, sin can creep in and ruins them, or the relationships becomes untrustworthy, dysfunctional, emotionally or physically abusive. These forms of love are depended on mutual acceptance, personality, physical attraction, compatibility, social status, position, age, sex, race, height, weight---preferences---relationships which are often prejudicial. These human relationships can change from hour to hour, one day to the next: A man is in love with his wife.

He finds out she's having an affair. He feels that he can't reconcile the marriage. The marriage goes before the judge in Divorce Court: Divorce is soon granted. What happened to the love? It was based on the condition that neither partner would cheat!

"We know that we have passed from death unto Life, because we Love the brethren"---1 Jn. 3.14.

Let us consider how much God loves us and calls us His children (1 Jn. 3:1). It is mind-expanding to believe and accept the Love of God. Not only did He forgive our sins but invites us to His House, to scoot a chair up to His grand dinner table and feast with Him in the bliss of Love, joy and peace. As His Bride, the Church is the object of His passionate Love. We are the Guest of Honor at the Wedding of the Lamb of God. As spiritually depleted and beggarly we were, now we sit with Him in the heavenly places.

The least we can do is spread the Good News of His Love to others. We have already thanked Him with our lips, but a life of Love speaks louder than words. A trustworthy sign that we have passed from spiritual death to spiritual Life is our Love for one another. Love is the measuring high hurdle and measuring rod. The difference between a babe in Christ--a Corinthian---and a mature Christian is the measure of Christ, the Love coming out of the vessel.

Love is the manifest evidence of the passing from one stage to another; without definite markers on this journey, how would we know where we are? We could be deceived into thinking our walk with Christ is progressing adequately and according to His divine schedule--when in fact we are still on the milk of the Word! John stated that Agape Love comes from God and there can be no darkness added to it. He wrote that Believers who demonstrate Agape Love are born of God and know God. Jehovah-Elohim commanded His Love towards us that while we were without strength Jesus Christ died for us. God deposited His treasure of Love in us so we would be capable of loving Him, our neighbor and ourselves. As there is no darkness in Love, there is no fear either. Those who are habitually fearful are not walking in Love.

When we walk in Love we are confident of God's grace and protection from Satan's attacks against us, our relationships, property and interests. We are not fearful of domestic criminals, foreign or domestic terrorists, sicknesses, diseases, poverty, or spirits producing fear. But if we say we Love God but hate our brother we're lying to ourselves and God. The Word states, we cannot Love God whom we have not seen and not Love our brother whom we see every day (1 Jn. 7-21). Remember, the Commandment is to Love God, our neighbor as ourselves. This Commandment should not be broken.

CHAPTER SEVEN

Secrets Of The Vineyard

"I AM the Vine, you are the branches. If any man remain in Me and I in him, he shall bear much fruit; apart from Me you can do nothing"---Jn. 15.5.

"But the Fruit of the Spirit is love, joy peace, patience, kindness, goodness, faithfulness, 23 gentleness, and self-control"---Gal. 5.22,23.

What distinguishes Christianity and Christians from the other so-called spiritual paths and their founders is the commonalty, the unity we share with Jesus Christ; in the other religions there isn't a merging of the many into one, no oneness in Spirit or destiny as is found in Christianity. Jesus Christ is God; God is capable of oneness, raising and converting the spiritually dead through Spirit Baptism into Eternal Life.

That is why He unites with us---to share His immortal Life with us. We became heirs to His famous and legionary Name. His Name was con-ferred on us by Grace through Faith the same way His righteousness was conferred upon us by grace through faith. In the highest heaven we sit and reign with Him. As long as we are part of the Elohim commonalty, we remain in Him.

Jesus speaks to every Christian when He says, "I AM the Vine and My Father is the Gardner." Every Branch that doesn't bear fruit Jehovah-Elohim cuts off; even if a Branch does bear fruit, He prunes and purges us by cutting us back so we will bear more and better quality of fruit the following ministry season. Believing the Word of God and being submitted to the discipline of the Holy Spirit prunes and purges us from dead works initiated by our self-life; we are often self---mentally and emotionally motivated and not God-motivated in the things we feel needs to be done to advance the Kingdom of God. Remember, the only works that please and are acceptable to God from us are His own works manifested via Anointing through us! The process of pruning is for our greater good and for the advancement of the Kingdom of God. The chastisement and correction we receive at the discretion of the Holy Spirit causes us to spiritually mature, as we remain attached to the Vine of Life.

The divine Gardener ministers to us, the Branches; we share in the Life of the Vine, who has everything we need stored in His roots, the Throne of God. When we realize our place and position in the grand theater of life, we can appreciate the humble spirit we become, a spirit who readily listens and submits to the guidance and discipline of the Holy Spirit's process of conforming us into the humanity and divinity of Jesus Christ, for the purpose of sonship.

Unproductive Branches are as good as dead; unproductive Branches are like religious people representing their belief system and not the Father, who is the Creator. They are like fire-wood thrown into the fire to fuel infernal Hell (Jn. 15:1-4). The substantial and surpassing worth of His discourse is for us to remain in Him. Jesus said that if—and that's a mammoth word—we remain in Him, He will remain in us.

No branch can bear fruit detached from the vine and laying on the ground; being separated from the Vine with His Life-giving rivers of living waters is a death sentence. Jesus is the Vine, and we are His Branches. We are not the branches of the Satan's vine, but Jesus' Branches, His Disciples, thriving in His Vineyard. Rotten branches may belong to the vine and be loosely attached to it; even so as some professing Christians may be tagging alongside with the true worshippers. We must be aware of their pretending and not be infected or affected by the disease of sin, doubt or unbelief; these three things are a rottenness to the Born Again human spirit; they can corrupt the fruit-bearing Branches and cause the local church to be unproductive in her witness. That's why the earthly gardener cuts the dead branches completely off. When the Vine bears much fruit, the Gardener is overwhelmed with glorious joy. When we bear abundant fruit it shows that we are responded to the Gardeners wisdom, appreciated His protection from demons, trials and tribulations, sicknesses and diseases; we appreciate His loving care and patience. Fruit are works; we're God's workmanship created in Christ Jesus to do good works. We're saved by grace through faith but produce works because we are saved. Not only are we saved, but have taken on the nature and characteristics of the Vine Himself. Again we must stress that the eternal counsel of Jehovah-Elohim and the commonalty, His plans, purposes and pursuits is to recover and restore the Earthbound Man, his lordship and dominion of the Physical Realm, that was lost because of sin; to find, convert and conform this fallen human spirit into the image and likeness of Jesus Christ, the Anointed One.

God isn't trying to make the fallen Earthbound Man the Messiah---He already has that Man---but to raise up a multitude of spiritually dead human spirits to stand on our spiritual feet and receive Eternal Life, our predestination. The Lord said that we didn't chose Him but He chose us to bear fruit. Bearing the fruit of his personality and character is the purpose in which He chose and placed us **In Him**.

Too long we've been bearing fruit---consequences of our evil heart---according to our carnal thought nature, which so happens to be the thoughts of the prince of darkness. We have, like the selfish citizens of Babel, been quite industrious at building our own tower and making a name for ourselves and the Devil in this world. Now, that wickedness must come to any end. God desires that we bear the Fruit of the Spirit to glorify His Name in the earth.

God through nature has orchestrated His own system for growth. Fruit doesn't grow on the vine but on the branches. The branches have to be fully attached and dependent on the nutrients of the vine; the fruit is colorful and highly visible---but the source of the fruit, the hidden life within the roots and vine is truly the fruit producer. The prepared, cultivated soil strengths the roots and the vine.

Therefore, the invisible life principle governs the production, the manifestation of visible and eatable fruit. No one with the naked eye can see the Spirit of Christ within us because the Spirit is invisible. Nevertheless, people can hear our words and see our lifestyle. Wouldn't it be simply marvelous if people hear the fruit of our lips as we sing praises to His wonderful Name? O bless the Name of Jesus!

"Be patient therefore, brethren, until the coming of the Lord. Behold, the husbandman waits for the precious fruit of the earth, and has long patience for it, until he receives the early and latter rains"---Jam. 5.7.

God, the heavenly Gardener sends the Holy Spirit early to water the Vine and the Branches. Tending the Vine is a labor of love, but the Branch requires His long patience and His latter rains of the Holy Spirit before He sees the results of His labor. His faith is such that He expects a good, hundred-fold harvest consistent to the nature of the Vine and His personal efforts.

The Gardener and the Vine work together to produce fruit that the Gardener can accept; rotten or sour-grape-servants will not be tolerated. The rains, the outpourings of the Holy Spirit help us to grow a sweet and juicy spirit. People will know that we're Christians by our Love for them and each other. We won't have to wear a sign on our back or tote a big Bible to impress or persuade people that we're sincere to the Person and teachings of Jesus Christ; our love for them will speak louder than words.

The Fruit of the Holy Spirit is really the Fruit of the recreated human spirit, because fruit grows on the Branch and not the Vine. These Fruit are the character of Jesus Christ, the Vine for which the Branch gets His Life. Our Fruit is slowly ripened on the Branch---this is called Sanctification---when the character of God is cultivated and nurtured in us as a lifelong process. God is patient; we have to be patient too. Our change will come.

The Potter's Wisdom

(627 B.C.) The Word of the Lord came to Jeremiah the Prophet. God told Jeremiah to go to the potter's house. Jeremiah quickly responded (Jer. 18.1). He expected to see a miracle, a suspension of the natural laws, something wonderfully created by the finger of Jehovah-Elohim. Instead he saw an old man laboring at his potter's wheel. Jeremiah looked around the room.

Certainly this wasn't what the Lord wanted him to see. On the shelves and tables, he saw hundreds of clay pots and vessels. Some of the vessels were large, small, short and fat; there were vessels for every use. But what really caught Jeremiah's eye was the craftsmanship, the beauty and creativity embroiled on many of the vessels; these vessels took a long time to complete; they had to be more valuable, even quite expensive. Jeremiah had seen these expensive vessels in the king's palace. Then Jeremiah noticed the less expensive vessels; these vessels were not as beautiful or imaginative; they were quite ordinary.

He reasoned that these vessels were for common purposes---perhaps a vase to hold a few wildflowers to grace the table of a farmer, shepherd or water for purification purposes. There were so many vessels in the potter's house. He thought that if the empty vessels were people, what would they desire to be filled with? He smiled at them: So many different kinds of unique and empty people longing to be filled! The potter supplied vessels to everyone.

Not only did he make new vessels but he repaired the old, cracked and stained vessels brought into the shop. Some of the vessels suffered terrible abuse! Out of the wine vessels he cleaned the difficult to remove stains and returned the vessels back into service looking just like new. The owners of the clay vessels needed the potter and his humble wisdom to know what to do to restore the vessels. No one knew more about clay that the potter. In the corner Jeremiah saw a large hammer.

He thought about Jehovah-Elohim: "Is not My Word like a fire? Says the Lord; and like a hammer that breaks the rock in pieces?" (Jer. 32.29). Beside the hammer were several badly chipped vessels. Jeremiah looked out the window into the potter's field. He saw a pile of discarded clay vessels hammered into small fragments; it looked like a pottery graveyard.

Now he knew the fate of the chipped vessels; because they were hardened and useless for service, the hammer was applied; they ended up in the pottery graveyard, because through severe abuse or neglect the vessels had fallen into such reproach that it wasn't practical or profitable for the potter or owner to salvage them.

Jeremiah saw that the potter's field was also the source of clay to make the vessels, and potentially millions of new ones. So it was fitting that from the ground the vessels were created and back to the ground they returned. Again his attention was focused on the potter. Jeremiah observed the vessel he was making was misshaped in his hand, so he compacted the moist clay and made it over again, working it into another vessel as it seemed good in his sight. The potter had mastery over the clay; to his touch the clay readily shaped. With wooden tools the potter made fine lines and details that made the piece unique; by certain designs and his personal trademark, people all over the world knew his workmanship from another craftsman.

At no time during the process did the clay cry out or complain, "why have you made me like this?" (Isa. 45.9). Then the Lord said to Jeremiah, "0 house of Israel, can I not do with you as this potter does? Says the Lord, behold, as the clay is in the potter's hand, so are you in My hand 0 house of Israel" (Jer. 18.6) (and Church). Now Jeremiah knew why he was at the potter's house.

It wasn't to see a miracle but to learn a basic truth: Israel (and the unborn Church in the womb) was to conform to the image of the divine Man who sits upon the heavenly Throne; the earthbound Man was being recreated to be a vessel of honor. Israel was marred and chipped due to her rough spiritual journey on Earth. Jehovah-Elohim, the Potter wanted to bring Israel into His house for repairs and cleansing from the contamination, corruption, acidity of life, and the old wine of idol worship; evil influences ate at Israel's sides and weakened the former foundation, so she needed to be stripped out.

Israel would become cleansed, consecrated and fit for the Master's use. God's House had different vessels for different purposes. Jehovah-Elohim, the Creator of all vessels was more than qualified to restore Israel than anyone else. Like the potter's wisdom concerning restoration of clay vessels, God has the greater wisdom to restore and revive His prized possessions. God actively seeks human vessels longing to be filled with Elohim-Life. He longs to be the new wine poured into freshly scrubbed vessels!

21"Does not the potter have power over the clay, from the same lump to make one vessel for honor and another for dishonor?

22 What if God, wanting to show His wrath and to make His power known, endured with much longsuffering the vessels of wrath He had prepared for destruction.

23 And that He might make known the riches of His glory on the vessels of mercy, which He had prepared beforehand for glory"---Rom. 9.21-23. Israel was the object of God's love; but the other objects, the targets of His wrath were the pagan nations. Because Israel was His chosen vessels, God showed them the wealth of his glory. Through His mercy He tolerated the sin of the other nations, and used them to chastise Israel. But afterwards the pagan nations paid dearly for their personal and national sin.

Again Jeremiah saw the graveyard of hammered clay vessels and another truth was revealed to him: These vessels were the objects of God's wrath and prepared for destruction. Rejected and unserviceable, they returned to the bone-yard. God is sovereign. Like the potter and the clay, God has absolute authority in how He applies Wisdom, Knowledge, Selection, Predestination, Election, Appointment or Calling. He is the Potter and mankind is the clay. God directs His wrath towards one people to show His love towards another people. God hardened the heart of Pharaoh:

"For the scriptures says to the Pharaoh, for this very purpose I have raised you up, that I may show My power in you, and that My Name may be declared in all the earth. Therefore, He has mercy on whom He wills, and whom He wills He hardens" (Rom. 9.17,18).

In the case of Pharaoh, God hardened his heart to create resistance to His demands. No one in their right mind would stand up to God in a fight to the death, so God, knowing Pharaoh's stubborn heart, arranged a situation favorable to Himself to display miracles and the awfulness of His wrath.

He purposed to deliver Israel in such a manner as to make a Name, a reputation for Himself among a people who didn't know Him from the Egyptian gods. If Pharaoh had given in too quickly, the deliverance would not have been as memorable. Today, for generations the Jews celebrated Passover. God's Potter House was a place of creation, restoration and love. There was joy, peace, mending of broken hearts and marriages, broken lives and dreams; there was forgiveness of sin and Salvation, the New Wine of the Holy Spirit. This and more was at God's Potter House.

The Narrow Gate

13 "Enter through the narrow gate. For wide is the gate and broad is the road that leads to destruction, and many enter through it. 14 But small is the gate and narrow the road that leads to life, and few that find it" Mt. 7.13,14.

The initiation into the mystery surrounding the Narrow Gate is revealed to those who hunger and thirst for righteousness. Jesus Christ is the Narrow Gate; He is the Way, the Truth, and the Life.

The Narrow Gate also represents Repentance and Faith in Jesus Christ, who is the Center of all things, the Alpha and Omega. In Christ Jesus, the Narrow Way, we discover all the treasures of heavenly wisdom, insight into His ways and purposes, knowledge and enlightenment. We enter in at the Narrow Gate and travel the Narrow Road, as we are led by the Holy Spirit towards Christian maturity. The Gospel of the Kingdom is preached on the mortal side of life. The Narrow Gate is Christ and the Heavenly Church; the Narrow Road is Christianity and the Earthbound Church, which is subjected to tremendous pressure.

The Earthbound Church and Christianity, being the entrance point for mortal man into the Kingdom of God, is being compressed, contorted, hidden by satanic deceptions and religions that were brainstormed in Hell, to create for mankind a stumbling block, spiritual blindness in those who are searching for a way out of slavery; this pressure is brought about by Satan.

It is intended to close the Narrow Gate and leave stranded billions of people who are candidates for Heaven. Satan wants only the Wide Gate open for mankind: The Wide and Broad Road of being conformed to the world, then spend the rest of eternity in Hell.

The Narrow Gate and Narrow Road can be compared to an EXIT sign on an interstate highway stating: "NARROW GATE EXIT HERE". In daily driving we may not be paying attention or driving too fast and miss the NARROW GATE EXIT on our first attempt. But usually there are other exists, other opportunities to leave the highway, double back, cross over and exist at the right place.

As we all know, Exits on an interstate are a lot narrower than the main highway; this is because not everyone on the highway wants to get off at the same exist, our destinations are different. Many of us motorists break the natural laws by speeding down the interstate highway of life until we get into a tremendous wreck. Because of the excessive speed and the fragility of our human body, the sudden impact is usually fatal: We did not exit the highway by our own will and now we are dead; through careless living and rebellion we missed the NAR-ROW GATE EXIT, and became eternally lost.

The riches of the treasures in Christ Jesus are deposited to our account, so that we can experience and distribute love, joy, peace, goodness and the other characteristics of Christ to others. By witnessing, giving our testimony of what the Lord has done for us, the Holy Spirit uses our witness to persuade the unsaved to leave the Broad Road of sin which leads to spiritual death, to obtain Eternal Life instead, and be joyfully acquitted of former crimes against God and humanity.

Hell has been enlarged (Isa. 5:14); it has acquired extra space to accommodate the harvest of the wicked **dead**: Multitudes, multitudes are in the valley of indecision, who cannot make up their minds to accept Jesus Christ. Hell is waiting for its fuel supply; like cords of dry wood the unsaved are tacked on the earth and destined to become fuel for the eternal fires of Hell.

Those who are predestined to be saved are at the moment on the Broad Road. For them the fullness of the time, their hour to accept Christ hasn't yet come. At one time we were all on the Broad Road. But when the grace of Jehovah-Elohim came into our mortal lives, our eyes were opened, our heart became fixed, our mind was made up, and we left the Broad Road.

The Broad Road and its Wide Gate also represents those of us who are trying to get to Heaven our own way. The Gate is wide to accommodate the huge rush hour traffic going into Hell---that spacious barren estate on the shores of the Lake of Fire. The Broad Road people are like Cain who offered to God what he felt God deserved. Cain offended God, disrespected his parents, who represented God's authority on earth. God, Adam and Eve told Cain that only the blood covered sin.

But the false philosophy and religion that was delivered to Cain from the bowels of Hell, spoke of a righteousness based on external rituals, personal works, mental and bodily discipline. Therefore, the Broad Road encompasses all the ancient and modern non-Christian religions and cults who, like the ministers of the ancient high places, shook their fist at the Throne, mocked with blasphemies against God and His prophets. The Broad Road ministers are the keepers of the Broad Gate on this side of mortal life; the Guardian of Hell is the keeper of the Broad Road Gate on the other side of eternal death.

Obviously, the Broad Road ministers are not ministers of Faith in Jesus Christ, the True Vine, neither has the Potter placed His distinctive mark on them. They think that they can lie, pretend and fool God like they lie, pretend and fool their followers, to believe that they are somebody important; but God cannot be fooled, neither will He place his Seal of Approval on their iniquity.

Why We Perish: The Broad Road with its multi-millions of spiritually blind souls is lined with the starved, spiritual corpses of those who are perishing; as the non-Christian, we perishing because we have not been fed the nourishing milk and spiritual food of the Word, which leads to Repentance unto Salvation. We perish because we have not been converted, regenerated into new creatures; we are perishing because we are in the bondage of sin. We perish because we are not seated with and in Christ Jesus.

We perish because our father is Satan and not Jehovah-Elohim. We perish because we do not have the abundant good treasure in heaven and within us. We perish because we have an abundance of wicked treasure within us, and don't want to exchange it. We perish because we are religious impostors, frauds, spiritually dead, having a form of godliness but denying the power of Christ.

We are perishing because we are trying to deceive God and sneak in the back door of Heaven, through a self-proclaimed prophet who rewrote the Holy Bible to deceive his followers into believing that Jesus cannot be both God and Man. As Broad Road travelers, we quote our favorite non-Christian scriptures, philosophers, psychologists, talk show hosts or others, as though they are an irrefutable authority on life and spiritual matters.

But all these reasons are but distractions, time-wasters, logical human excuses to remain on the Broad Road. The Broad Road activists believe and teach that all spiritual paths lead to Heaven; that's like saying that all interstate highways lead to Alabama; so how can all religions lead to Heaven? In these religious paths, where are the evidences that God is involved---the signs, wonders, healings and miracles? But we experience the Anointing, the Resurrection Life of Christ operating through the cross of Jesus in the Church and Christianity.

The Apostle John proclaimed: "He who has the Son has Life and he that has not the Son has not Life" (1 Jn. 5.12). John saw and experienced the Spirit of Jesus as Life, and **In Him** is no darkness, no evil at all. Jesus is the Way, the Truth and the Life, because no one can communicate with the Father or go to Heaven except by and through Him. Jesus is the Guardian of the Narrow Gate.

Jesus said, "I AM the Door; by Me if any man enters in, he shall be saved" (Jn. 10.9). The Door, the Gate, the Way are all the Narrow Gate and Road that leads to Life, and few there will be that find it. As we travel down the Broad Road, Satan and his spiritual terrorists are deployed there. His army of devils are camouflaged, hiding among the surroundings using it as cover. They ambush us every chance they get. Whenever possible, they get ahead of us and plant land minds on the Road in our pathway.

Their goal is to kill or seriously wound us through slow deaths like sicknesses and diseases, alcohol and drug abuse or other forms of sin, before we make the decision to exit for Christ and Heaven. They know that if we continue to speed or cruise down the Broad Road and pass up opportunities to leave the Broad Road for Christ, that eventually, since we have limited life-fuel, we will run out of mortal lifetime and come to a screeching halt, or get to the end of the Broad Road where there are no more Narrow Gate Exits.

Then suddenly, we hear a blood-curdling scream, and, discover that it was our horrified scream; life is over. We have lost the most valuable possession we had---our soul!

18 "And a certain ruler asked him, saying, Master, what shall I do to inherit eternal life?

20 You know the commandments...21 And he said, All these have I kept from my youth up. 22 When Jesus heard these things, He said to him, Yet **you** lack one thing: sell all that you have, and distribute unto the poor, and you shall have treasure in heaven: and come, follow Me.

24 And when he heard this, he was very sorrowful: for he was very rich.

26 And they that heard it said, Who then can be saved?"---Lk. 18.18,20-22,26.

The rich young man asked Jesus how he could have the Life that he perceived the Teacher had. It was obvious that the man saw the demonstrations of Elohim-Life, the manifestation of the Word of God as Jesus' words released Spirit and Life. The young man wanted that Spirit and Life as his own.

This man was also described as the "rich young ruler," which implies that he was a man with political and religious authority, a lawyer, perhaps the son of a prominent elder of the Twelve Tribes of Israel; the young man was likely a member of the Sanhedrin Council. But one thing was certain---his heart was empty and he wanted what Jesus' has; he wanted to experience and be confident that Jehovah-Elohim was his Father.

As a youth, he believed he had done all that the Mosaic law required of him; he also did what the religious leaders taught him: He went to the temple, paid his tithes, kept the Sabbath holy and was zealous after the traditions of the fathers. He sincerely believed that his lifestyle justified him asking Jesus for Eternal Life based upon his self-effort.

Jesus examined him, loving him, He guided the young ruler through the Commandments. Jesus knew that all have sinned and come short of the glory of God; Jesus also knew that no one but Himself ever fulfilled the Letter and Spirit requirements of the Law. Yet, here was a young man believing that he had kept the entire Law. A man may keep the outward form, the religious aspect of the Mosaic Law, but the Sovereign Lord Jesus desired him to live in and practice the Spirit of the Law.

Jesus spoke to him of love, kindness, compassion, honesty, integrity, generosity, selflessness, obedience and the willingness to give up everything for Christ, exchange it all for the heavenly treasure of Eternal Life. Jesus looked into his heart and saw the spirit of pride, his self-treasure; then He prescribed the medicine: To sell everything, give it to the poor, then come and follow Him through the Narrow Gate to the Narrow Road that leads to Eternal Life. This idea was madness to the young man; parting with his riches and given his inheritance to a bunch of sinners was asking too much! In his eyes, if the poor were not so ignorant of keeping the entire Law, they would be like him---rich.

The young man wanted the Life of Christ, but he was not willing to humble himself, lose his pride, his vain spirit, and obey the Master in this last instruction: Be loosed from the bondage of materialism, the love of money, because his heart was chained to his wallet. Instead of him using his money, his money used him, keep him on the Broad Road; Satan spoke through his money and now the young ruler believed that money was more important than Eternal Life. Perhaps, the young ruler didn't realize how much he loved his money until Jesus told him to divorce it; then his money personified and spoke distinctly to him and said: "Leave this Jesus and go back to the marketplace!"

The spirit of greed was hidden in the young man's heart. Jesus challenged it, exposed it to the Light of His Word. Then the disciples and people asked, "Who then can be saved?" Now another misconception was exposed: The people also believed that the rich were blessed and were entitled to Heaven and Eternal Life, but the poor were cursed, and therefore weren't entitled to the same benefits. Jesus taught them, "The things which are impossible with men [as saving himself by social status or works] are possible with God." Eternal Life has nothing to do with us being rich or poor, but is a matter of Faith in the finished work of Jesus Christ at Calvary. Yet everything that is sacrificed or donated towards the Kingdom of God, shall be multiplied in our lives here on earth and in the world to come (v. 27-30).

We can all learn a valuable lesson from Jesus' conversation with the rich young ruler, and even the lessons revealed in the Old Testament: In the Old Testament Books of the Law and the Prophets, were writing the prophetic Word of God. These words describe the future realities of things and events; the prophets and priests didn't themselves possess these realities, only types, shadows and visions of them, promises and words only.

Until Jesus incarnated, lived, taught, died at Calvary, resurrected, was Glorified and sent back the Holy Spirit, we were not spiritually or mentally ready to accept and receive revelation, interpretation, understanding and doctrine for the Throne of God, in order to be competent to preach and teaching the Word of God. The Secrets of the Vineyard and the Potter's Wisdom would have escaped our mental apparatus in favor of more visible and material substance. If not for the help of the Holy Spirit, the wisdom of the Broad and Narrow Road would sound as foolish as Jesus telling the rich young ruler to give away his money!

The Holy Spirit arranges divine appointments, giving us the rare opportunity to acquire personal experiences **In Christ**, with other people, world situations and circumstances. The Holy Spirit accelerates our Spirit-filled Life **In Christ Jesus** by bringing us into the depths of wisdom, knowledge, and spiritual insight in His ways, plans, purposes, and Who the Savior is, whom we are **In Him**, while He helps us to pray, wills to speak and exert His influence in the world through us.

In Him Is Life

1 In the beginning {before al time} was the Word (Christ), and the Word was with God, and the Word was God Himself.

· 3 All things were made and came into existence through Him.....

4 In Him was Life, and the Life was the Light of men.

5 And the Light shines on in the darkness, for the darkness has never overpowered it {put it out or absorbed it or appropriated it, and is unreceptive to it}"---Jn. 1,3,4,5 (Amp. Bible).

Previously, we endeavored to discover the Secrets of the Vineyard and the Potter's Wisdom. Now we will explore the Person of the Vine and God who is the Vinedresser and Gardener---the One who cares for the Vine and Branches.

The natural vinedresser not only prunes, but lifts the natural vine off the grown and supports it with wooden stakes to keep the vine from rotting against the earth, and thus enabling the grapes to receive ample sunshine; he also places a fence around the vineyard to protects the vine from the little foxes (demons) that would tear down and destroy the vine and grapes for food---and also to be mischievous! Apostle John in explaining who Jesus Christ, the Vine is, began with, "In the beginning", which is the correct place to start when talking about this kind of Life. He wrote that before all time was the Word, who is also the Person called Christ. This Christ was with God as a member of a Trinity (Father, Son, Holy Spirit). Yet, all things were made and came into existence through Christ.

It was **In Him** that this (Eternal) Life exists, and the Life could lift and restore fallen persons---us, to the heights of heavenly dignity and fellowship with the Father, the Vinedresser, as though we had always been with Him and never were separated because of sin.

The Light is the radiance, the offshoot of the Life of God. The Life of Christ is the same Life that keeps God and the other members of the Trinity alive; this Life is what makes them eternal: Omnipotent, Omniscient and Omnipresent---God. The Life of Christ is so powerful, the darkness, Satan and his demonic government has never over-powered the Life, or quenched the Life---nor is he capable of benefiting from the Life, use the Life or redirect the Life; in fact, since his fall from Heaven, Satan cannot even understand how the Spirit of Life even works (because the Spirit of Life is also the Person called the Holy Spirit).

And thus Satan wars against God and the intelligent Spirit-Life that flows from the Throne of God and Christ, as Christ supplies the needs of those who call upon His Name.

Apostle John further testified as a witness concerning the Light, that all men through him might believe: That the Light, Life, Word, Christ was incarnating into the world of human beings as a human being, and whosoever believes in Him, trust in and relied on His Word, would have the authority, right and rank on earth and Heaven, to be called sons (and daughters) of God.

Believers would receive His Life-Spirit, inward likeness and character that is in the image of God. They would receive Him in their once dead or unresponsive human spirit; by a quickening, being made alive and conscious by the Life-giving Presence of the Holy Spirit of Christ. And once being conscious and awakened, the human spirit would once again be aware of its Creator, love Him, praise and worship Him, communicate with Him, and assist Him in His overall plan for the redemption of mankind.

The Word became flesh, a human being known as Jesus of Nazareth. He pitched his tent of flesh, tabernacle and made His abode among us. The entrance of the Word brought Light (Ps. 119.130). The Word brought understanding and intuition, the ability of the human spirit to "know" without studying the will of God, His plans, purposes. Jesus said in John 8.12

"I AM the Light of the world; he that follows Me shall not walk in darkness, but shall have the Light of Life. Here the Savior, as John did, used the terms Light and Life to emphasize that the radiance of the Light is in proportion or direct relationship to the Life that is within; that because the Spirit of Christ dwells within us, there should be corresponding fruit or evidence of His Presence.

Jesus also says it this way: "Ye {we} are the Light of the world. A city that is on a hill cannot be hid. Neither do men light a candle, and put it under a bushel, but on a candlestick. Let your Light so shine before men, that they may see your good works, and glorify your Father which is in heaven." When we receive the Holy Spirit in our human spirit, a transformation and awakening takes place; our spirit is awakened from its slumber and filled with the radiance, Light and Life of Christ.

Once empowered, we walk the earth as new creatures (unregenerate people are human spirit, soul, and physical body or three-part beings. Christians are Holy Spirit, human spirit, soul, and physical body or four-part beings---a new creation. So, Jesus was saying, with all this Light and Life within, don't hide the Life but do good works so that the Father will receive glory and others will want what we have.

"Therefore if any man be in Christ, he is a new creature: old things are passed away; behold all things are become new" (2 Cor. 5.17).

This is a familiar scripture to many and quoted widely. We are new creatures because we have God's Spirit dwelling in us and we belong to His family. We are no longer the plantation slaves of the world, but have been given the ministry of reconciliation. We are ambassadors for Christ, and we are to persuade people to come out of the darkness and demonic activity into the Light and Life. The old Egyptian slave mentality, even the grave clothes of the past, must be shed at the Jordan River or left in the tomb as Lazarus' stinky grave clothes.

The Battle of Life continues. The enemy of our soul, though he tried to kill us many times, failed in those attempts and we made it by the Grace and Mercy of God. The prayers of other Christians and the protection of the guardian angels; our angels of God who fight many unseen battles, are often overwhelmed by the magnitude of assaults, the hordes of evil spirits executing maneuvers and operations between Hell and on earth.

Because of evil spirit activity, many of our family members and neighbors perish on the Broad Road before they make up their minds to accepted Christ, the Life; and others, motivated by demonized flesh, kill themselves with drugs, alcohol, hazardous lifestyles and never find Christ, the Vine.

But now that we are children of God, the enemy has stepped up his attacks. As fugitives from the world system, we have dared to defy the ruling spirits over the geographical area in which we live, not to mention the thousands of demons and people they use to keep the sin going in and around us. We have declared war against the enemy of our soul! Jesus said in John 10.10, "The thief comes not, but to steal, and to kill, and to destroy: I Am come that they might have Life, and that they might have it more abundantly."

The thief, meaning Satan, was a murderer from the beginning. When he comes to steal, he is not really after our material possessions, though he may play mind games by interfering with our finances---but his real goal is to enslave our soul and to keep us away from God. His goal is to return us to the former state before we received the Life of Christ. He doesn't want us to have the abundant Life, whereby we worship God. No, he is not after our 72 inch color television or our new car---he wants our worship and conformity to the world.

"And be not conformed to this world, but be ye transformed by the renewing of the mind, that you may prove what is that good, and acceptable and perfect will of God" Rom. 12.2.

This is just one of many Scriptures that instruct us that there is something evil and severely wrong with the world system of thought, belief and behaviors. The Word also refers to "former conversations," the stuff we used to talk about and places we used to go because it was important to us. The flesh, or the mind of the flesh is called the "old man" who is corrupt and deceitful and full of unredeemable qualities.

The flesh cannot be rehabilitated, improved, "churched," shamed into behaving or changed by mental health experts---except drugged until harmless and also senseless. It has to experience death at the cross, so the "inner man" of the heart can make himself known; staying on the vine until ripe safeguards us from dangers.

In this crooked and perverse world, we are to shine as Light and Life to the world; the demonic powers dissuade us daily, and we must continuously take a stand for Christ and the Life He has instilled in us. As the fruit of the Vine, we are more than conquerors!

Who Is the Son of Man?

"27 And beginning with Moses and all the prophets He explained to them the   things concerning Himself in all the Scriptures. 11 For the Son of Man is come to save that which was lost"---Lk. 24.27; Mt. 18.11.

Although Jesus of Nazareth was born in Bethlehem, Judea, the Christ **In Him** was from the beginning. Christ, the Word was with God as God. Jesus spent many hours with His disciples explaining that He is the incarnation in human form, the Creator of Heaven and Earth. He came unto His own people, the Jews and humanity as a whole, and they didn't recognize Him or believe that He was the owner of this Vineyard.

This was mainly because Satan told them that he was the rightful owner and could distribute the land to whomever would be an obedient servant to him. What Satan said was not the whole truth: The Son of Man came to make war, to defeat and take back the Vineyard for the Vinedresser, Jehovah-Elohim. Yes, the Son of Man came down from Heaven to seek and to save what was stolen from Jehovah-Elohim in the Garden of Eden. Not only was God's family corrupted and shanghaied, but the earthbound Man lost his authority to rule the creation. In this are several substantial and compelling reasons why countless millions of truth seekers past and present Christians, from generation to generation, all over the world believe that Jesus Christ, the Son of God, the Son of Man is the **only** Savior of the human race. It is not only the fact that he made the claim, "I am the Son of God" (Jn. 10.36) that convinces everyone that He is who He says.

The people who lived during the terrestrial walk of Jesus were probably more skeptical that we are today. The Jews received the Word of God through Abraham the Hebrew who was born in Ur of Chaldea. He in turn taught it to his sons, and the Word of God found place in the hearts of humanity.

So for centuries the Jews were familiar with the Word, scriptural promises and prophecies concerning the arrival of the Messiah, the Anointed One. And though there has arose many false prophets in the Old Testament and New Testament Church (even in the Body of Christ today) the true seekers of God are always able to recognize them. We as creatures born in sin and conformed to the world have been implanted with iniquity---the desire to do what is wrong, even if we don't actually do it.

We are prone to lying, manipulation, control and many have claimed that God or an angel appeared and commissioned them to do a work for them (many serial killers claim that God told them to punish "certain" sinners.) But in Israel these "messiah" impersonators or impostors relied on black magic, self-promotion and bribery to gain power and authority over their listeners. Yet the statements of Jesus of Nazareth were not only backed up with Scripture that could be read and confirmed, but miracles, signs and wonders.

Even after His death at Calvary, He continues to reach back from beyond the veil where He sits on the right hand of God, to perform even more miracles, signs and wonders through the Holy Spirit who indwells the true followers of Jesus Christ; and this is accomplished through a tangible, super-spiritual medium called Faith. No other religion, philosophy or their founders and leaders has ever accomplished this; neither has any of them raised from the dead to further lead their disciples. The claims of Jesus Christ were backed up by His lifestyle: Although the majority of the Pharisees and Sadducees who made up the official Sanhedrin Council didn't agree, violently, and with murderous intent opposed Jesus' claim to be the Messiah, they didn't state, because they had no evidence, that He was a criminal wanted by the law or lived an immoral lifestyle; that He was lazy and wouldn't work, or that He was a beggar; that He was unlearned and ignorant of the Scriptures or even out of touch with Jewish traditions; but they did believe that He was a prophet greater than John the Baptist, a scholar, teacher and the leader of a new sect. Jesus has a unique character and lifestyle.

He lives a holy lifestyle because He is holy; and so in the days of his humiliation as the Son of Man, He praised and worshipped the Father in Spirit and in Truth; He loved and honored His mother; His love for souls was and still is insatiable, in that He watches for and pursues after the lost; and rejoiced over His disciple's ministry successes, but grieved over those who refuse to come to Him for rest. He is The Prayer Warrior in that He is also the Priest of the Heavenly Sanctuary.

He is meek, gentle, humble, compassionate concerning the sick whom He heals. He was and remains intolerable of demons and the evil works perpetrated against humanity; He drives them out with His Sword, the Word of God. With greater detail, God definitively pointed out the Messiah. In His pilgrimage, He was altogether other than any man---past, present or future.

The specifics of this Man is found in the Old Testament, a legal document written over a few thousand years; it contains more than 300 references to His coming. Using the science of probability and mathematics the chances of just 48 of these prophecies being fulfilled in one person is 1 followed by 157 zeros! Therefore, the Old Testament Scriptures are 100% accurate, God-inspired and true. It is by Faith and reasonable thinking that Jesus Christ is the Messiah and all the other titles that He laid claim to.

He fulfilled the Old Testament prophecies concerning Himself, to the extent that He read to others about Himself. No one person could possibly fulfill all those prophecies---not even a hundred-man team of the best actors or magicians could successfully fulfill one of God's prophetic promises, that He has willed and spoken to come to past in the earth hundreds of years previously. These prophecies not only directly affected the citizens in the cities where they were given, but every nation to the end of the ages!

Here are a few of the testimonies: Jn. 1.34 "I have seen and testify that this is the Son of God."--- John the Baptist; 2.11 "...miraculous signs Jesus per-formed in Cana..." --- Apostle John; 3.2 "...no one could perform the miraculous signs you do..." --- Nicodemus; 9.16 "How can a sinner do such miraculous signs? --- Pharisees; 11.47 "Here is this Man performing many miraculous."--- chief priests; Lk. 4.34 "I know who you are--- the Holy One of God!"--- unclean spirit; 4.41 "You are the Son of God!"--- unclean spirit.

Miracles, miracles and more miracles; these were not magic tricks or carefully orchestrated hoaxes. Human being who witnessed the miracles, signs, wonders, healings and deliverances testified to them. The Pharisees, priests, Romans---and even demonic spirits (who usually lie and it would have been to their advantage to say that Jesus was an impostor) shrieked in terror because Jesus is indeed God in a human (now glorified) body.

And when an enemy says something positive about a person, it must be true. These miracles also prove that God the Father placed His seal of approval on the works of Jesus Christ; if Jesus was an impostor, God would never in a billion years raise Him from the dead. In Genesis 3.15, God said to Lucifer that He would raise up the Seed that would crush Lucifer's head: It is done!

Seated In Heavenly Places

Another benefit of being attached to the Vine is fellowship: Therefore Imagine that we are sitting on the Throne in the highest Heaven with Jesus Christ. Not only us personally but all Christians are sitting with Him, and spiritually **In Him**. Our other two bodies, the Soul and Physical Body are situated in the two lower realms where Satan operates; those parts of us also yearn to be set free in Glorification.

The spirit part of us, the part recreated in the image and likeness of Jehovah-Elohim, sits In Jesus Christ, and whatever our Soul Body binds or looses on earth—we from our heavenly seat In Jesus Christ, agree from the Throne in Heaven. From this perspective and position far above the demonic government, we exert our authority over Satan and his government. Our duty and concern as Christians isn't to spend unnecessary time wrestling with demonic forces or being overly concerned with the Territorial Spirit Rulers above us, but to fight the good fight of faith. We don't run around hunting demons in the city---like the actors in the demon movies---but spend quality time being a witness for Jesus Christ, giving testimony that Jesus is the Son of God and Savior of the world; we spend our time cleaving to the Vine, reading the Word, praising His Name, worshipping Him in spirit and in truth.

Occasionally, depending on our Calling and ministry, it' becomes necessary to confront and cast out demons, to bring healing and Deliverance, by exercising our authority In Jesus' Name, from our heavenly position In Christ. By Faith, we expect the demons to come out of people; we expect sicknesses and diseases to vacate their human hosts. The Anointed Word of Faith accomplishes miracles. In response to our prayers and authority as one seated **In Him**, Jesus Christ commands the Second Floor entities, the Territorial Spirit Rulers, to obey according to the great Name He possesses. Jesus Christ will demand changes in the operation of the Second Heaven in response to our united prayers; when the Christian Denominations in the Physical Realm are in total agreement with the Word of God (including accepting Apostles and Prophets), major changes will happen in the world; Jesus is ready. Changes are made on an international, national, state, city and community level through Intercessory Prayer.

Christians with the boldness to pray downwards from our heavenly seat, instead of praying upward from our earthly position---and call those things that be not as though they were, are the Lord's intercessors and world-changers. As Born Again Believers we are present and conscious on all three floors, tiers, levels, heavens or realms of life; the unsaved are not present or conscious at the Third Heaven.

Their human spirit and soul are combined, and bound to the lower heavens, the world. Jesus Christ is present on all three levels of life; therefore, our High Priest can use our Human Spirit, Soul, and Physical Body as His instruments to advance the Kingdom of God. We are the Body of Christ on earth; we are capable of having the blessed Mind of Christ. Jehovah-Elohim made us a three-in-one-entity, because it pleased Him. From a spirit's point of view, this world seems illusionary; a spirit--

-clean or unclean---isn't subject to material boundaries, gravity or other natural obstacles. Therefore, this world and those who live in it appear to be easy prey to the unclean devils. The Battle for Life, to stay in and on the Vine of Christ Jesus rages on; our minds are the battlefield. We are daily bombarded by sinful thoughts, voices, temptations, seduction and visible lures to persuade us to sin against God, to leave the protection of the Vine and Gardener.

The Demonic Kingdom specializes in wholesale misery, sin and immorality. Our prayers are hindered by our participation, conformity to the wide world of sin: The lust of the eyes, the flesh, and the pride of life. Even our Physical Body, a pleasure-oriented creature, is one of our worst enemies.

5 "For it is impossible [to restore and bring again to repentance] those who have been once enlightened, who have consciously tasted the heavenly gift and have become sharers of the Holy Spirit.

6 If they then deviate from the faith and turn away from their allegiance--[it is impossible]to bring them back to repentance, for (because, while, as long as) they nail upon the cross the Son of God afresh [as far as they are concerned] and are holding [Him] up to contempt and shame and public disgrace"---Heb. 4.5, 6.

Another way that Satan's Second Tier Government prosecute their war against Jesus Christ is by indirectly attacking Him through His Earthbound Church Body. As the Salvation Plan of God, includes Sanctification---the changing us into His image---is being implemented and Christ is being revealed in us, evil spirits step in to lure us away from God; they depress, oppress, obsess, but can't possess a Christian.

Their goal is to make our life difficult, so difficult that we give up and detach ourselves from the Vine. Yes, we as Christians can be oppressed, tempted by the seduction of demons spirits; we can be bound by obsession to tradition, legalism, formalism, sex, phobias or materiality; but we can't be possessed, that is, 100% owned by Satan because at the Spirit Level we are seated **In Jesus Christ**; we sit in the Third Heaven far above the influence and access of Satan.

The only way Satan and his cohorts can inflict devastating harm upon us is persuade us to denounce Jesus Christ as our Savior, denounce the Word, Name, and Blood of the Atonement; then we intentionally walk away from our Salvation and go back into sin and the world, as though we were never Born Again. Jesus said that He would never leave us or forsake us; but it is free-will possible that we can leave Him and forsake Him, walk away from our Salvation or even our ministry Calling, just like many of us have walked away from our careers, spouse and other responsibilities.

Therefore, the theory of "once Saved always Saved," as some of us were taught, is incorrect doctrine; it originated from preachers who, needing Inner Healing and Deliverance from trafficking in iniquity, instead moved to Scripturally justify through rationalizations that they cannot lose their Salvation no matter how abominably they sin. If we have walked away from Jesus in a permanent backslidden state "it is impossible" to be restored, as long as we daily crucify Him, hold Him up to the world as though making a statement that He is found not worth of our praise and worship; we hold Him up to contempt and public disgrace—especially to those who knew that we were once a Christian, a minister of Jesus Christ.

28 "And so since they did not see fit to acknowledge God or approve of Him or consider Him worth knowing, God gave them over to a base and condemned (reprobate) mind to do things not proper or decent but loathsome.

29 Until they were filled (permeated and saturated) with every kind of unrighteousness, iniquity, grasping and covetous greed, and malice. [They were] full of envy and jealousy, murder, strife, deceit and treachery..."---Ro. 1.28,29 (Amp.).

We as a Christian have known the Lord Jesus Christ and have became a partaker of the Holy Spirit, have decided to go back into the world, with the multitude of unsaved people who refuse to accept Jesus Christ as their Savior. In either case, the Spirit of God whose purpose in the earth is to bring us to Jesus Christ and change us into His image, will after a period of trying to convince us to return, or to get Saved, will allow us to do and be what we want to do and be---thus turning us over to Satan.

As former Christians, Satan will continue to use us to traffic iniquity and ridicule the Name of Jesus until we become as reprobate as he is. There may come a time when the Holy Ghost calls it quits in our life because we reject Him, grieve Him, and His revelation knowledge of Jesus Christ. Being grieved and rejected, the Holy Spirit leaves because He has no legal right to occupy our human spirit without our permission; yet, if we have denied Him while under the influence of sickness, accident, mental illness or amnesia---forgotten about Him, the Holy Spirit knows the true heart of everyone.

But for those who intentionally left Him for the love of the world, an once-Saved person, would undoubtedly revert back to our originally unsaved self-life---except for an important distinction—we are now a reprobate, subject to condemnation, the Curses for Disobedience, a habitation for every unclean and hateful demon—even a candidate for complete 100% possession by demon spirits. It has been reported by Christians who have received revelation about the conditions of Hell, that there is a place in the lower levels for former Christians—they receive extra punishment! Again, staying on the Vine is wisdom for Eternal Life:

By being carnal, worldly minded we leave ourselves open to unclean devils; unless we're willing to denounce the works of darkness in exchange for the Love and Light of Christ, our faith and prayers will be hindered, and our position **In Him** will do us no good; we'll continue to struggle in prayer as though always climbing a rugged and steep mountain. As long as our mind operates in this fallen world and our soul is un-restored, we'll have to deal with, one way or another, Satan, demons, our flesh and the world.

Our spiritual rebirth took place in the Third Heaven, the realm of the Spirit. This level wasn't available to us until Jesus Christ died on the cross, arose from the dead, ascended into Heaven, whereby He opened up the windows of Heaven and poured us out the Blessing, that there isn't room enough for us to receive it all. These are the Secrets of the Vineyard with Wisdom of the Potter's House. Be Blessed!

CHAPTER EIGHT

The Church Needs Apostles & Prophets

"Surely the Sovereign LORD does nothing without revealing His plan to His servants the prophets" ---Amos 3.7.

The battle of and for Life began in Genesis. In Chapter Six the record of the calling and commissioning of Noah was found. Noah was the first of God's prophets. God called him to deliver His prophetic Word to a people who enjoyed riotous, wicked living, a people who refused to walk by faith, but instead walked by human impulses, emotions, human knowledge and eye sight.

Noah obeyed God and built an ark, which is also a symbol of the ark of safety that is found in the loving and protective arms of the Messiah. Being in the ark is being In Him, and having no righteousness of our own but having an imputed righteous that is by Faith in Jesus Christ. Noah's ark was like the boat that the Twelve Apostles rode in when the storm came.

Jesus was also in the boat. The Lord got up from His rest, and rebuked the storms that were in the lives of those in His ark of safety. God, who because of the lawlessness of mankind, in His divine Judgment and indictment, extended His mercy towards mankind for 150 years by allowing Noah to preach and prophesize the coming destruction of the entire world; yet God would not lift a finger to execute His will until He first revealed His plan to the Prophet Noah. In Genesis Chapter Twelve, the story of Abraham began.

In it Abraham was called of God. He left his kindred, to go to a place that God later show him. God revealed His eternal plan to Abraham, that Abraham was (already in His eyes) the father of many nations, and that the entire world benefited from the Promise and Blessing; this Promise and Blessing was the Seed, Jesus Christ; the

Messiah, the Holy One of Israel who crushed the serpent's head. Abraham believed and trusted in the words of God and his faith was counted to him as righteousness. Abraham became a friend of God, and he also became a prophet of God.

 "And the LORD said {to the destroying angels}, Shall I hide from Abraham that thing which I do; seeing that Abraham shall surely become a great and mighty nation, and all the nations of the earth shall be blessed by him?" (Gen. 18.17,18).

Here again is an example of how God elects to work through and with those who are His prophets (and New Testament Apostles) before He will do anything substantial, that would affect the course of a nation, society, human history and experience (especially His New Testament Church). Throughout the Old Testament, whenever civilization declined to the point that the righteous Judgment of God conflicted with His Mercy, God raised up deliverers like Moses; Judges like Samuel, Samson, Deborah and others.

He also sent prophets to the people to intercede---from Noah too John the Baptist---to persuade Israel, the children of God, to repent and turn from their wicked, flesh and idol-worshipping ways. God first sent the Word to the king of Israel. The king was responsible for the spiritual, moral, economical and social welfare of his subjects. But more often than not, the kings "did evil in the sight of the Lord," and refused to listen to the men of God. When the king could have been a good example of godly Light to the people, they chose to remain in total darkness.

By doing so, they consented to slavery rather than defending Israel from slavery; they led the people who admired and trusted them further into darkness than perhaps they would have went on their own. (The same is the situation today with our political leaders). God raised up and called good and faithful men like Isaiah, Jeremiah, Ezekiel, Daniel and others into the vineyard to preach the Word and intercede---stand in the gap between Him and the people. But again the Children of Israel, the unborn Church, refused to abide by the Word of God. But in direct response raise up their own false prophets and teachers to tell them what they wanted to hear, and not what they needed to hear from the Lord. They loved the darkness more and rather than the Light of God's truth. They enjoyed the revelations of the sensual flesh, the whispering in their itching ears, and pseudo visions during their sleep---the fellowship of the territorial demons; they loved it more and rather than the sweet Holy Spirit of Love. And so, they murdered the Truth-bearing prophets, and preferred religious slavery over the abundant Life. Therefore, the Old Testament closed with a 600 year silence, until the birth of John the Baptist who prepared the way for the Lord Jesus Christ.

New Testament Church

19 "The household of God...; 20 And are built upon the foundation of the apostles and prophets, Jesus Christ, Himself, being the Chief Corner Stone"--- Eph. 2.19,20.

Jesus Christ, our Lord and Savior is no different towards His Apostles and Prophets. Even in the days of his humiliation, He discussed with His Apostles the details of His mission, death, burial, resurrection and Exaltation. He also told them that as His Father works, He works; because He and the Father are One.

Jesus told Peter that upon the revelation that Peter had, that Jesus is the Christ, that He would build His Church, and the gates of Hell will not prevail against it; and even though the Earthbound Church may stumble off the path into one ditch or the other, the powers, influences or strategies of the territorial spirits will not quench the Light of Christ, or drive the Light from His Church; because the Church is built upon a unique foundation:

The Apostles and Prophets, with Jesus Christ being the cornerstone---the stone that determines the direction and square of the building, and is inscribed with the date it was laid. The Twelve Apostles of the Lamb were those who walked with Jesus during His earthly journey. After Jesus ascended, He send back the Holy Spirit to indwell Believers (Acts 2), and blessings of Ministry Gifts :

"It was He who gave some to be apostles, some to be prophets, some to be evangelists, and some to be pastors and teachers.

12 To prepare God's people for works of service, so that the body of Christ may be built up,

13 until we all reach unity in the faith and in the knowledge of the Son of God and become mature, attaining to the whole measure of the fullness of Christ"---Eph. 4.11-13.

Satan pulled out the stops to put an end to the ministry of Jesus Christ. He thought it was a master stroke to kill Him, so he could carry on business as usual. He worked feverishly manipulating the Jews and Roman authorities to accomplish his goal: To murder the Prince of Peace. Of course, he was not discerning to know that it was the plan of God all along to sacrifice His Son.

When Jesus ascended on High, He sent the (Five-Fold) Ministry Gifts designated to continuously, throughout the ages, buildup and strengthen the Church, the Body of Christ. As stated early, two of the Ministry Gifts are part of the foundation of the Church: The Apostles and Prophets. The Apostle is a New Testament counter-part to the Judge of the Old Testament (like Samuel), and the New Testament Prophet is not sent to Israel alone, but has a broader function---even to the nations of the world.

Again the enemy stretched forth his hand to vex the church: He has convinced many denominations that the Church doesn't need a complete foundation---that it doesn't need Apostles or Prophets in order to function until Jesus returns; that the Apostles and Prophets were only necessary to start the church with doctrines, signs, wonders and miracles, but all that is past!

Most Christian denominations accept the ministries of the evangelist, pastor and teacher, but refuse to recognize and accept the Apostles and Prophets as being necessary and a vital part of the whole, the Church. But they dare not say they don't need the third part of the foundation---the Chief Cornerstone, Jesus Christ, for fear that they would be labeled non-Christian.

If our car had a six cylinder engine and it was only running on four cylinders, we would experience a severe lack of horsepower; it wouldn't run efficiently at all; and if it was missing two spark plugs, thus leaving to open holes in the engine where they belong, it wouldn't start at all. This is the situation in most churches: A lack of anointing, a lack of miracles, signs and wonders; a lack of power over the flesh because of the lack of Ministry Gifts; the Apostles and Prophets are also given to function in the local churches. Where the two vacancies are, the enemy has two open doors to come and go as he wills; Satan will also pull members of our congregation out through those empty places, and out of the protection of the church, where the Apostles and Prophet are supposed to be posted. The evangelist, pastor and teacher are readily accepted worldwide. But the offices of Apostle and Prophet are being defined and accepted in the Charismatic, Pentecostal, Full Gospel and Nondenominational churches.

The "ascension gifts" are biblically given; they are needed for the Church to fulfill its destiny here on earth. "For the perfecting of the saints" was the kind intent of the Lord Jesus Christ in giving the gifts. If the Church did not need them, He wouldn't have given them. We miss out on the fullness of the measure of Christ, the yoke-destroying power of a well-oiled (anointed) and maintenance church, without the presence and impute of the Apostles and Prophets; two ministries that are directly anchored to the Lord Jesus Christ, the Chief Cornerstone.

To refuse something or someone whom Jesus Christ has given to help us is not unlike the children of Israel who refused the Prophets and even killed them. We may not physically kill an Apostle or Prophet, but we refuse to listen to them and even assassinate their character by running our mouth against them, by spitting venom with our acid words of contempt and spiritual pride; our own ignorance being fueled by the same spirits who persecuted the Prophets in the Old and New Testament; then we wonder why we have so many issues, health problems, barren and are not growing spiritually or even materially!

Jesus is called the Chief Apostle (Heb. 3.1). He is also called Prophet (Mat. 21.11), Shepherd (Gr. Pastor), and Teacher (Jn. 3.2). He also is The Evangelist (Jn. 4.4). Having in Himself the Five-Fold Ministry Gifts, He delivers to the Body an expression of Himself spread out over the entire Body, but uniquely concentrated (as are the Spiritual Gifts that accompanies these offices) in these five offices. If we, like in our secular employment, had an office that is given to us by our employer; and this office has all the equipment, computer technology including an inexhaustible reference library, we would get more work done there than in our home, or walking down the street. So it is with the Ministry Gift offices that are empowered with Spiritual Gifts and direct access to the Employer. We as Apostles and Prophets can accomplish more for Christ.

"In reading this, then, you will be able to understand my insight into the mystery of Christ, which was not made known to men in other generations as it has now been revealed by the Spirit of God's holy apostles and prophets"---Eph. 3.4,5.

Apostle Paul, who wrote two-thirds of the New Testament, stated that the mystery of Christ has now been revealed through the Apostles and Prophets; he did not say through the evangelist, pastor or teacher---but through the Apostles and Prophets. It stands to reason that the Apostles and Prophets receive a greater degree of revelation knowledge than the other gifts, through the other gifts are important in their duties to make up the fullness of the Body.

Paul wrote this several decades after Jesus had resurrected and ascended; he was not talking about the Old Testament Prophets, though they did receive abundant revelation of Christ, but the New Testament Apostles and Prophets, in whom the mystery of Christ was revealed. Apostles and Prophets are to continue throughout the Church Age, until "we all reach unity in the faith and in the knowledge of the Son of God and become mature, attaining to the whole measure of the fullness of Christ" (Eph 4.13).

"Husbands, love you wives, just as Christ loved the Church and gave Himself up for Her to make her holy, cleansing Her by the washing with water through the Word, and to present Her to Himself as a radiant Church, without stain or wrinkle or any blemish, but holy and blameless"---Eph. 6.25-27.

The Churches Needs Apostles & Prophets

Has all the Church members reached unity? Has all Church members acquired the knowledge of the Son of God? Has all Church members matured? Has all Church members achieved the whole measure of Christ? Are all Church members without stain, wrinkle or blemish? Has the sons of God been revealed? Has Jesus come back for His Church? The answer is NO!

The Earthbound Church is not complete, therefore the sons of God are not yet revealed (Ro. 8.19-23). The Five-Fold Ministry are to operate in the Body of Christ on earth until the second Advent of Jesus Christ. At which time the sons of God will be revealed; mortality will be changed to immortality, and then the Five-Fold Ministry Gifts will not be needed because we will be complete, "to wit, the redemption of our bodies" (Rom. 8.23)---made perfect through Glorification, which is the completion of the Holy Spirit's process of Sanctification.

The word "apostle(s) occurs 85 times in the New Testament but is not mentioned in the Old Testament, meaning that the Apostle is a gift of the Dispensation of Grace; it is an office and person approved and appointed by Jesus Christ as is evident in the four Gospels of the appointment of the Twelve Apostles, and later Luke writes of Matthias replacing Judas Iscariot as an Apostle (Acts 1.15), Paul, Barnabas (Acts 13.1) and others were sent out as Apostles.

The word "prophet(s)" occurs over 150 times in the New Testament, about 20 of these references refer to Prophets in the Church age after Pentecost. The word "teacher(s)" occurs 125 times in the New Testament. The word "evangelist(s)" occurs 3 times in the New Testament. The word "pastor(s)" occurs 1 time in the entire New Testament (Eph.4.11). Surprisingly, the word "pastor(s)" is used in the Old Testament more. So how is it that the local churches today place more attention on the office of pastor and evangelist, when the Apostle and Prophet is clearly mentioned more?

The word "pastor" is mentioned once, and the word "teacher" being used even to describe non-Christians. Consider the numbers:

Apostles, Prophets or teachers total approximately 200 times, while, pastors and evangelists have a combined total of 4 times! It really doesn't make a lot of sense why the majority of Christians do not believe that there are or should be Apostles and Prophets in the modern Church.

This is the results of exclusion by the local church pastors; it is religious persecution, prejudice, fear, ignorance, control and the insecurity of local pastors who are convinced---deceived by the church-dividing spirits---that the Apostles and Prophets would come into their church to tell them what to do, or steal some of their tithing members (many pastors don't care about non-tithing members leaving), or expose the religious nonsense that is being taught.

The offices of Apostle and Prophet are different, though one compliments the other; both the Apostle and Prophet have Spiritual Gifts and receive divine revelations. Because of this, the local pastors shun and even discourage us from communicating with these gifted saints, and often discourage these Ministry Gifts from being a part of the local congregational church.

The pastors fear that the Apostle and Prophet would undermine their authority and challenge their decisions; so they often teach us that there are no Apostles or Prophets in the modern church, and if they claim to be such—and we listen to them, we are disobedient and some type of God-sent punishment would befall us; it is as though they try to curse us.

Many pastors are very insecure about their position in the Body of Christ, and use manipulation and other psychological maneuvers to maintain control over the thoughts and actions of those of us they believe personally belong to them. Pastors refuse to allow these men and women access to their pulpits to teach or preach the full gospel, in hope that they would get discouraged and leave the local church (or even the entire city).

Sometimes the pastor may purposely humiliate, anger make light of the Apostle or Prophet to create a hostile environment in order to find something to hold against them for the purpose of discrediting their ministry and personal credibility before the congregation or board members. Then they stick out their chest and say, "I told you that he wasn't an Apostle. Did you hear what he said to me?!" Apostles and Prophets are not perfect; plus demon and human attacks are more frequent and severe on them.

Characteristics & Ministries

"Enter ye in at the straight gate: for wide is the gate, and broad is the way, that leads to destruction, and many there be which go in there: 14 Because strait is the gate, and narrow is the way, which leads unto Life, and few there be that find it"---Mt. 7.13,14.

The Apostle is called of God and not by men; a true Apostle is not called by proclaiming himself or herself an Apostle, but by revelation and confirmation by Jesus Christ, and through the agency of the Holy Spirit, since the Holy Spirit speaks on earth and in the Church in behalf of Jesus Christ. Neither does a pastor, evangelist or teacher have the authority to make anyone an Apostle, when they are not themselves an Apostle: Apostles beget Apostles, as pertaining to the ceremonial setting apart the Apostle:

The Holy Spirit shares the Chief Apostle title with Jesus Christ, the two being one Spirit. The characteristics and ministry of the Apostle (root means "sent") is always in revelation to the foundation of Christianity. Even in the Old Testament era, when Israel was over-taken by their enemies or strayed away from the path to worship false gods and doctrines, Jehovah-Elohim raised up Judges to lead them out of the physical and demonic bondages.

Even so, are the Apostles sent forth to set the congregation, the Church free from the bondages of false doctrines that have infiltrated into the Earthbound Church. When the local churches have lost the True Way, grope and feel around in the darkness---a darkness and blindness demonically imposed---the Lord raises up Apostles to lead the church, out of the right or left hand ditch, back onto the Narrow Road.

God also raises up Prophets to prophesize to us words of warning, faith and encouragement to those who are in religious captivity. In the battle for Life we sometimes find ourselves off of the Narrow Way and treading the muddy bottom of a religious ditch, dug for us by none other than the territorial demons and those human being who are their willing and unwilling servants.

But we also know that no one individual other than Jesus Christ has all the following characteristics without measure. The below list is also a composite of characteristics found in the New Testament Prophet. The measure or degree of anointing and gifts depends on God's plan and purpose for our life.

Characteristics

Acts 2.4 Apostles are **filled with the Holy Spirit;** Acts 2.14-36 Apostles **preach the Word of God;** Acts 3.1-8 Apostle **Heal the Sick;** Acts 4.1-12 Apostles are **persecuted;** Acts 5.1-11 Apostles pronounce God's **judgment;** Acts 5.12 Apostles work **signs and wonders;** Acts 8.14-17 Apostles **lay hands** on others to be filled with the Spirit; Acts 8 Apostle are founders of **new churches and ministries;** Acts 10 Apostles are sent to preach in **other nations;** Acts 14.23 Apostles **ordain pastors and elders;** Acts 15.1-21 Apostles settle **doctrinal disputations;** Acts 16.18 Apostles cast out **demons;** Acts 19.22 Apostles **Send forth other Apostles** to minister; 1 Cor. 3.10

Apostles are master builders who lay **spiritual foundations;** 1 Cor. 4.14-15 Apostles give **warnings** of pending judgments; 1 Cor. 7.1 Apostles counsel pastors and answer biblical questions; 1 Cor. 11.34 Apostles set **churches in Kingdom Order;** 2 Cor. Apostles **edify the Body of Christ;** Eph. 2.20 Apostles are part of the **Foundation** of the Church; Eph. 3.3-5 Apostles prophesize and receive **revelation** directly from God. Mt. 22.14 "For many are called but few chosen."

Calling & Commission

The purpose of this study of Apostles and Prophets is to reveal the relationship between the absence of the two offices of Apostle and Prophet to the decrease of authority and power in the local churches, a decrease in the ability of pastors to live the supernatural and moral Christian lifestyle before God and the world; and the effect that it has on the evangelists who brings the people to the pastors to be nurtured in what is supposed to be a safe, loving and spiritual environment, but often turns into a religious, controlling, manipulative, deviant and sexual pit that does more harm to the young Christian than good.

The absence of the Apostles and Prophets from the foundation opens the door for demonic activity. Such a tremendous absence ties the hands of the Prayer Warriors and Intercessors, from pushing back the forces of darkness that come against the local churches.

The huge hole left in the protective shield surrounding the church, is an open door to every seductive and hateful spirit to twist the minds of pastors until they are exposed as weak "sinners" before the finger pointing world, and those Christian haters. Those who love the darkness more and rather than the Light of Christ would proclaim, "That's why I don't go to church---the pastor is a hypocrite! He is an alcoholic who sleeps with prostitutes!" In the natural realm, the information they have is the truth, but not the whole story on that pastor's life. If the haters could walk in his shoes for a year they may have fallen even further than he did. Apostles and Prophets provide more power to the Body of Christ to walk in Authority, Holiness, Righteousness, Truth, Healing and Deliverance.

Another problem that is facing the Body of Christ is a sudden appearance of false prophets and false apostles. Whenever there is the real thing, whether in the secular business world or the Christian Church, we will discover that the counterfeiters want their piece of the action. In the case of the local churches, the territorial spirits create such confusion that we don't know who to listen too---who is the real or false apostle or prophet?

We will know them by their fruit! The Calling and Commissioning of the true Apostle or Prophet in the Christian Faith is not based on self-promotion, church board hierarchy promotion, human worthiness, persistence in prayer, or petitioning God for assignment; and there are no modern day Apostles or Prophets of God outside of New Testament Christianity.

The prophetic ministry of John the Baptist was the last of the Old Testament genuine Prophets of God. Prior to the Exaltation of the Lord Jesus Christ, the arrival of the Holy Spirit to seal and indwell Believers, and the unique New Testament Covenant mantle placed upon the Apostle and Prophet, the remaining Judea prophets either converted to Christianity, or eventually died under the Old Covenant.

Jesus said in John 15.16, "Ye have not chosen Me, but I have chosen you, and ordained you." This is based on God's Sovereignty, Election, Predestination and Calling, in that He chose---before the foundation of the world---Apostles and Prophets (and other members of His human family) to serve Him in this capacity as special ambassadors.

"Though He were a Son, yet learned He obedience by the things that He suffered. And being made perfect, He became the author of eternal salvation unto all them that obey Him"---Heb. 5.8,9.

To whom much is given, much is required; therefore, the Apostle has to undergo and learn discipline: Obedience, faith, prayer life, morals, integrity and biblical doctrines. As the Word states that Jesus learned obedience by the things that He suffered, and was made perfect though His obedience, the Apostles and Prophets are made complete and competent by a wide range of life experiences, in which wisdom is gained through spiritual, intellectual, emotional, and often traumatic experiences;

That all things may work together for the good, to create empathy for the struggles of the lost and downtrodden, the beaten-down ones who have lost their way; to create keen perceptions of what is needed in the stand against the ruling spirits; to convert humanity to Jesus Christ, and buildup the Body of Christ for His return. The Apostles and Prophets are required to hear from God more accurately than the other members of the Body of Christ, to reveal God's specific Word, will, plans, purposes and pursuits.

We should not take it lightly to call ourselves Apostles or Prophets just because we have the gift of prophecy (which is a Spiritual Gift not the Office of Prophet), organizational skills or are good at administrative functions; there is more to these offices than that--- including Christ-likeness. The Apostle Paul states the correct attitude, the centrality of Christ in the thinking of the Apostle and Prophet: "But whatever was to my profit I now consider loss for the sake of Christ. What is more, I consider everything a loss compared to the surpassing greatness of knowing Christ Jesus my Lord, for whose sake I have lost all things. I consider them rubbish, that I may gain Christ and be found in Him, not having a righteousness of my own that comes from the Law, but that which is through faith in Christ. I want to know Christ and the power of his resurrection and the fellowship of sharing in His suffering. "(Phil. 3.7-10).

There is more to being an Apostle or Prophet than someone telling us in a prophetic conference that we are, reading books on the subject, or even going to theological school and graduating with a Doctorate Degree. Bible college is a great way to obtain biblical knowledge; but biblical knowledge and the Calling of God are not the same thing, though God may send us to school as preparatory.

Paul writes of forgetting about our own accomplishments or failures---be they past or present---and embrace the attitude of pursuing and obtaining Christ, the High Calling of God, and count everything else as rubbish (King James Version says dung), and put an end to self-promotions, self-glory, self-will and self-preservation; to suffer loss of the love of the world and all that is in it, for everything that God has called us to; and press purposely and upward for the mark of the prize of the High Calling in Christ Jesus.

Many are called, but few chosen (Mat. 22.14). Like the Special Forces Units of the United States Army, many solders try out for this elite group, but few actually complete the rigorous training to become America's Best. So, many Christians receive the high calling and ignore it; others receive it and don't want to go through the preparation; still others, having become religious, worldly and self-centered, have the wrong attitude, and therefore never press pass the Calling stage to the Commissioning stage.

And yet there are even some Christians who are Called but have not been released as Apostles or Prophets, but have gone out on their own---and therefore are not "sent" ones but "went" ones. Being unprepared, these Christians do more harm than good because people see their obvious rough edges, lack of discipline, lack of integrity, scanty Bible knowledge and no anointing; hence, no miraculous, signs and wonders accompanying their ministry.

By their inexperience and bad behavior, they prejudice the local churches from listening to the Commissioned and seasoned Apostles and Prophets. There can be a lengthy time between the Calling and Commissioning. Bible examples of God's process for taking us from Calling to Commissioning varies.

Patience is a Virtue

Abraham was called at age 50---after 50 years Abraham progressed from Calling to Commission; Joseph waited 13 years before he saw a   partial fulfillment---then he had 80 years of successful leadership and ministry; David waited 17 years for a partial fulfillment of the prophecy---then he had 40 years as king of Israel.

Elisha waited 12 years as an apprentice of Elijah--- then he had 50 years of prophetic ministry; John the Baptist waited 30 years for his Commission, and it lasted about 2 years before he was executed--- Jesus said of him, born of woman, that John the Baptist was the greatest of the Old Testament prophets; Jesus of Nazareth waited 30 years for His Commission, and it lasted about 3 ½ years before He was crucified---now He has an eternal ministry as Head of the Church, King of Kings and Lord of Lords.

The Twelve Apostles went through 3 ½ years of training, but Judas Iscariot was not Commissioned because he betrayed Jesus and then hung himself; Apostle Paul waited 17 years; his ministry lasted over 30 years.

God's preparation process applies to all who are Called; but to be Chosen is to finish the course and keep the faith until released and Commissioned. We cannot be like Judas Iscariot, who betrayed Jesus for 30 pieces of silver, later to find his neck in a noose and hanging from a tree; we cannot allow our Calling to be cut short through greed or love for the things of the world; we kill the Calling by being impatient, rebellious or lifted up in pride.

Accountable To The Call

29 "For the gifts and calling of God are without repentance {irrevocable}."

19 God is not a man, that He should lie; neither the Son of Man, that He should repent: has He said, and shall He not do it? Or hath He spoken, and shall He not make it good?

20 Behold, I have received commandment to bless: and He hath blessed: and I cannot reverse it"---Ro. 11.29; Nu. 23.19,20.

The Apostle Paul stated very passionately of how he pressed towards the mark for the prize of the High Calling of God. With this press comes a tremendous responsibility and accountability to the Caller and Calling. Once the Calling of God is made plain to us, it is our spiritual duty to receive the Calling, and place ourselves under the guidance of the Holy Spirit and the human leadership that He chooses.

In the same way that we didn't choose our natural parents, nor did we choose Jesus as our Lord and Savior---He chose us---we do not chose what spiritual parents that the Holy Spirit places us under. Sometimes God chooses a certain individual mentor or group of mentors as in a Bible College. Anyway, we are account-able to be obedient to the Caller, the Call, and our spiritual parents, if we want to grow in Grace and knowledge.

All Christians have a Calling; it may not be Apostle or Prophet but nevertheless it is a legitimate Calling. We cannot escape the responsibility of God's Calling, because it is irrevocable, binding and cannot be rescinded not even by Him. God will never change His mind on this matter.

He is a purpose-driven God who calls purpose-driven people. God sometimes adds to the Calling by broadening it to include other areas of ministry, but not take from it, unless a certain season within the Calling is completed; an addition to the Calling is not a second thought, but a season of the original Calling that we did not yet know about. He will also provide the Spiritual Gifts, finances and support staff necessary to navigate and be effective within the Calling.

God is the same way with Spiritual Gifts; it is the reason that we see Christians who have fallen into some manner of sin but still minister in their Calling with active Spiritual Gifts: God will not cancel the Calling or take the gifts; but He might take the Christian home instead!

Mt. 28.19,20 states: "Go ye therefore and teach all nations....teaching them to observe all things...Mk. 16.17,18 states: "These signs shall follow them that believe; In My Name shall they {meaning us} cast out devils....they shall lay hands on the sick and they shall recover."

These verses are associated with the Great Commission; and the Great Commission applies to all Christians. All Christians have a basic Calling to witness about Jesus Christ. We can invoke and use the Name of Jesus Christ to activate our Spiritual Gifts, to heal the sick, cast out devils or counsel the downtrodden and broken hearted.

Being faithful to this basic Calling on our life will advance us, make us available and able for our major life Calling; in that we are faithful in the smaller things, God will advance, promote and propel us into greater things. As the Apostle Paul recounted his conversion experience to King Agrippa, in Acts 26.13-19, he said "....I was not disobedient unto the heavenly vision."

We discover by reading the scriptures, that Paul didn't start out being an Apostle though he had the Calling on his life. Paul started out as a new convert, a babe in Christ, who needed Ananias to pray for the healing of his blind eyes and activate his destiny. As Paul obeyed the Call, the Holy Spirit led him through many stages of development---the process. Paul was patient and didn't fight the process, as some of us do, but allowed the process to change him from Saul to Paul; it was more than a mere name change, but a character and personality change---to the mind of Christ.

Then we see in Acts 13.1: "Now there were in the church what was at Antioch certain prophets and teachers; as Barnabus....and Saul (Paul). Here we see Paul is spoken of as being either (or both) a prophet or teacher, two of the Five-Fold Ministry Ascension Gifts.

He was progressing in his Calling. Paul was elevated to the status of prophet-teacher, when at the end of the meeting, the Holy Spirit spoke audibly: "...separate Me Barnabus and Saul for the work I have called them" (Acts 13.2). The men, who heard the command of the Holy Spirit, laid their hands on Barnabus and Saul: These men where now "sent" ones, and from that day forward were called Apostles: "Which when the apostles, Barnabus and Paul, heard..." (Acts 14.14).

The Holy Spirit promoted them to their high rank in the Body of Christ. For this same reason we should not take it upon ourselves to be called Apostles or Prophets. The Holy Spirit cannot use self-promoted but God-appointed people. This is also a reason why our ministries fail: For one, we are not Called into the particular ministry that we have; and two, we are not prepared, released by the Holy Spirit, and demons overwhelmed us.

"I have finished the course and kept the faith," is what Paul declared in 2 Tim. 4.7. In order to finish the course we have to know what it is! Many of us don't know what our Calling is. The Holy Spirit will reveal it to us if we ask in sincerity---but once we get the answer we dare not go to the office supply and have them print up business cards (as most of us do), but we humbly ask Him what to do next. As stated earlier, the Holy Spirit will place us under a human mentor; it is not likely that He will teach us personally like He did with Paul, seeing that there are now millions of Spirit-filled Christians around us and in the Body of Christ Body of Christ that He has been using for decades. Those of us who say, "all I need is Jesus and the King James Version Bible!"

We are deceiving ourselves to believe that Jesus doesn't use His human Five-Fold Ministry Ascension Gifts to edify the Body of Christ. He also uses the other saints and Bible translations; plus Jesus didn't speak the King James 1611 English, because in his area Greek, Hebrew, Latin and Aramaic was spoken (however, being God, Jesus can speak any language He needs to.).

Jesus Christ, our Commander and Chief, equips us before sending us into battle. The weapons we have are not physical but spiritually mighty through God to pull down of strongholds, expose and uproot a well-entrenched enemy. That is why He places us under a "Commanding Officer," a Ministry Gift. Many of us miss our Calling because we are too proud to study under someone else.

This leads to anger, resentment, rebellion and we even leave the mentor to be free from the appointed authority which is a part of our appointed destiny. The desire to be free from authority, covering, the mentor and his local church, and to start our own ministry, leads us to prematurely call ourselves a "seasoned" Apostle or Prophet (or prophetess)---when we haven't completed our training, nor been released by the Holy Spirit. We go along for a season, or even thirty years, until the cycle comes around and we reap what we sow!

The Dispensations

"Having made known unto us the mystery of His will, according to His good pleasure which He has purposed in Himself.

10 That in the **dispensation of the fullness of times** He might gather together in one all things **In Christ**, both which are in heaven, and which are on earth; even **In Him**"---Eph 1.9,11.

The dispensations of God involve enormous expanses of time. Though our plans may be in consideration of several years, God's overall Salvation and redemption plan encompasses eons of time called dispensations.

A single dispensation of God is actually a period in which God accomplishes certain things to further His ultimate goal; in each dispensation He has predestinated, Called and Commissioned certain individuals to play an important role in that dispensation. In the present dispensation, the Apostles and Prophets are needed to fulfill the plan of God for the Church; without the Apostles and Prophets, the foundation of the Church, the plan of God continues, but is not completed until the fullness of the dispensation and counsel of His will is accomplished.

Declaring the end from the beginning, in the ages o come, Jehovah-Elohim showed forth the Dispensations of the Counsel of His will.

The first dispensation was the **Dispensation of Angels**, the Ante-chaotic Age, from the Creation of the Earth to chaos (Gen. 1.1,2); angels ruled in the Pre-Adamite Era; the test and purpose was obedience to God while ruling under Him. Lucifer and one-third of the angels failed the test, and were cast out of Heaven with no hope of redemption. The age ended in judgment, destruction, Lucifer's Flood and eternal damnation for the fallen angels and the humanoid race(called by science, the Cave Man), who possessed angel-like spirits instead of the human spirit of Man.

The second was the **Dispensation of Innocence**, the Ante-Diluvian Age (Gen. 1:3-8; 14), from the Re-Creation to the Fall of Man. The test and purpose was Obedience and Faith while in the state of innocence; Adam and Eve failed by eating of the Tree of the Knowledge of Good and Evil. The results was judgment and the Fall of Man, judgment of Lucifer and the Curse; and the Promise of Redemption of Man by the Messiah.

The third was the **Dispensation of Conscious**, the Ante-Diluvian Age (Gen 3.22-8.14), from the Fall of Man to Noah's Flood. Length of time 1,656 years. The test and purpose of God was: Since Man knew the difference between good and evil, to follow his conscious as directed by God's Word. Man failed by moral acts of murder, idolatry, false religions, cults etc. The results was Judgment and Noah's Flood; provisions for redemption was Noah's Ark, and Sheol, also called Paradise, the temporary abode of the dead.

The fourth was the **Dispensation of Human Government**, the Present Age (Gen.8.15-Rev.19.10),from Noah's Flood to the call of Abraham. Length of time: 427 years. The test and purpose was for Man to obey the laws of human government, rule with faith and honesty, punish wrongdoers and worship God. The dispensation allowed Man to obey God's Word under a new provision of conduct: Man's government with God's laws. Noah and mankind failed. The results was Judgment; tongues confused and civilization divided. The provisions for redemption was the sacrificial offerings.

The fifth was the **Dispensation of Promise**, the Present Age (Gen. 8.15-Rev. 19.10). Length of time: 430 years. The test and purpose was for Man as a member of Abraham's Family of Faith, to believe the promises of God and obey the gospel of the Abrahamic Covenant. Abraham, Isaac, Jacob, and mankind failed; the results was Judgment upon Israel and Egypt. The provisions remained the continuous sacrificial sin offerings, and afterlife in Sheol.

The Sixth was the **Dispensation of Law**, the Present Age (Gen.8.15-Rev. 19.10), from Exodus to the Preaching of John the Baptist. Length of time: 1,718 years. The purpose was that Man was given the Law until Christ, the Messiah arrived. The test was for Man to obey 2,713 Commandments, judgments and ordinances of God; and for Man to realize from personal experience that he was a sinner, couldn't by his own will or strength be righteous and keep the Law; and therefore failed to please God by works, deeds or self-righteousness. Man failed to live by the faith-based Abrahamic Covenant, and was given a law-based Covenant. The results was failure by the Israeli people. Judgment fell upon Israel and the world. The provisions for redemption was the cross of Jesus Christ.

The Seventh was the **Dispensation of Grace**, the Present Age (Gen. 8.15-Rev.19.10), from the Preaching of John the Baptist to the 2nd Advent of Christ. The purpose of God was to call out His chosen, predestined one, the Church from out of the world. The test was whether His children, through obedience and faith, would forsake the pleasures of the world to be found In Him, with a righteousness based on faith in the revealed Word of God. Israel, the early Church, and the Church today had fallen short of God's expecttations. The results was Judgment in the Church and on Church officials, and the wrath of God poured out on the nations of the world; often the protection of God removed. The provisions for redemption: The Blood of Jesus Christ.

The eighth is the **Dispensation and Rapture** of the Church, the Present Age (Gen. 8.15-Rev. 19.10), Period of time: At least 7 years before the End of the Dispensation of Grace (Mat. 3.1-Rev. 19.10). The Rapture consisted of Jesus Christ coming for His Church, the Bride. The Rapture and Second Coming are two separate events; first Jesus comes for the Saints, then He comes back with the Saints. The Rapture takes place before the Tribulation. There are no signs of the Rapture; only signs of the Second Coming of Jesus Christ, the Messiah. The Rapture is the Blessed Hope of all Christians.

The ninth is the **Tribulation Period**, the Present Age (Gen. 8.15-Rev. 19.10) The Beginning of Daniel's 70th week to the Second Advent of Jesus Christ. The timing of this was at least 7 years after the Rapture. God's purpose was to judge Believers concerning their works and to burn unfruitful works. God gave rewards for faithful service. This Dispensation was also to fulfill prophecies and bring Israel to repentance and faith in their Messiah. The formation of the ten kingdoms and the rise of the Antichrist ushers in the Tribulation period. The 7th Seal, 7th Trumpet Judgments, and the 7th Vial Judgments take place. Then the Marriage of the Lamb, the 2nd Advent and the Battle of Armageddon.

The Tenth is the **Dispensation of Divine Government**, the Age to Come (Mat. 12.32, Eph. 1.21); from the 2nd Advent to the New Heavens and New Earth (Rev.19.11-20.15). This is also called the Millennium. The length of time is from the 2nd Advent of Jesus Christ to the New Heavens and New Earth. The purpose of this dispensation is to restore righteous and eternal government on Earth as it was in the beginning when angels ruled. Still multitudes of people followed Satan to the end: Fire from Heaven devours the wicked. Satan, the Beast and fallen angels are confined to Hell. Jesus Christ reigns supreme.

The Eleventh was the **Dispensation of Faithful Angels and the Redeemed**, the Age of the Ages (Eph. 2.7,3.11). The length of this Dispensation is Eternity. The purpose of God is to complete the counsel of His will, to carry out His eternal plan.

Now there was no further need of testing: The Saints of God are perfected. God continues forever using the Saints and faithful angels to rule Creation.

"Having made known unto us the mystery of His will...11 who works all things after the counsel of His will"---Eph. 1.9,11.

As stated earlier, the local churches are like so many engines that have two of their sparkplugs either missing or incapable of delivering a spark. If missing, the church-engine will not start at all; and therefore if the passenger-congregation wants to go someplace, human beings have to push the church-vehicle; this is the situation in many churches:

Human personalities (and demon spirits) manipulate and push the church along through gimmicks, fund-raising schemes, entertainment, celebrities and music. On the other hand, the church-engines may have two sparkplugs (so-called apostles and prophets) that are present but not delivering a spark. In this case, they are false apostles and prophets; people with these high titles but no Calling, and therefore no Anointing. In this case, the local churches lack power, stall out and occasionally stop; it is also difficult to started Sunday mornings. The Apostles and Prophets are the foundation and remedy to the powerless and underpowered churches!

Notes

www.ingramcontent.com/pod-product-compliance
Lightning Source LLC
LaVergne TN
LVHW051055080426
835508LV00019B/1893